STEPPING INTO A LIFE OF JOY

Dear Shannon,
May your life
be full of lots of
love and laughter
Love,
Suzanne

Revised Edition 2018

ISBN-13: 978-0-9861581-1-7

Stepping Into a Life of Joy

One woman's journey from misery to mastery
using the Law of Attraction

by

Suzanne C. Young

Dedication

This book is dedicated to all the people in the world who are searching for a life of joy but don't know how to find it, and especially to my beautiful niece, Theresa (Tracie) Elizabeth Custer, who passed away June 18, 2015.

What Readers are Saying

In everyone's life there are defining moments which chart the course of the future. These moments don't come often, but when they do, your reality changes forever. Sometimes you look back and realize the effect each had upon you. Little did I know on a sun-filled morning in June of 2011 that one of those defining moments would occur. It was the morning when I first sat down with Suzanne Young. That conversation and many since then, not only provided paths to achievement, but also led to inner discovery and understanding the mysteries of my universe.

In *Stepping Into a Life of Joy*, we learn about Suzanne's evolution from a person with little self-respect to one who deserves your utmost respect. It is an honest, genuine, unabashed account of one's lifelong transformation. Even though I encountered Law of Attraction previously, I never really understood how to implement its principles. Suzanne provided the travelogue, so I could rendezvous with my desires… and accomplish much more than I believed was possible. She showed me the life-changing process which positively impacts me every day. And the beauty of it all, as Law of Attraction would attest, is that Suzanne continues to create and expand in joyous ways.

Paul Flancbaum

Suzanne does a beautiful job of helping you make the connections between what is happening in your life and how you are impacting (and/or co-creating) it with your thoughts and beliefs. While she shares the painful aspects of her experiences, she doesn't wallow in them. She shares her heart, her understanding of her role, then takes you by the hand and steps into her joy with you as witness. This is an effective way of blending the delivery of empowering information with an act of friendship and love. Bravo Suzanne! And more importantly, thank you.

Leah Beck

Stepping into a Life Joy clearly demonstrates Suzanne Young's teaching and coaching skills. She recalls the most vulnerable aspects of her life while sharing the lessons she learned from each of them. Her writing is visual and clear, and she tells her story without malice or self-pity. She recalls painful and life changing events while accepting responsibility for creating them. She truly has learned how to *step into a life of joy*, and her book will inspire all who read it.

Nancy McDaniel, Certified Personal Trainer/Formula for Fitness

Suzanne's journey is a familiar one. Many women, and men, will identify with the raw, painful beginnings on her path of self-discovery. The pivot to self-enlightenment that Suzanne makes along the way is the intriguing twist in this story. Part biography and part Law of Attraction primer, *Stepping Into a Life of Joy* gives us all not only hope for a happier journey, but shows us how to incorporate practical, life-changing methods, resulting in a life filled with ease, love and JOY.

Susan Green, Passionate Proofreading

Beautifully written - honest and courageous outpouring of the heart.

Loree Sims

When I read *Stepping Into a Life of Joy*, I was totally surprised! I've known Suzanne for many years and she never once mentioned how unhappy she was in either of her marriages. I had NO idea how much pain she was going through. Over 20 years of seeing each other at the annual UndercoverWear conventions (a home party plan we both joined in 1980-81) she was always smiling and appeared happy. Reading her book helped me understand why women stay with abusers and I applaud Suzanne for her strength and determination to overcome all the fear and uncertainty of not one, but two divorces, and move forward. I'm delighted she figured out why her past unfolded as it did and what she needed to change within herself to stop the pattern of attracting abusive relationships. Suzanne introduced me to the Law of Attraction and we always have fun exchanging Law of Attraction stories every time we talk on the phone. I continue to be amazed at and impressed with Suzanne's resilience and determination to take charge of her life and always look forward to hearing the next successful step in her wonderful new *Life of Joy*.

Emily Gardner

Table of Contents

Foreword

Every woman has dealt with adversities in life. It's not the challenges that make one strong – it's how one handles those challenges. In this book, Suzanne Young skillfully takes us on a journey about not only her personal struggles but also the difficulties we all face as we go through life.

As women, we try to understand, and we try to accept. Yet, many times we are compelled to make changes. As I have often said, "Change is difficult, but change is good, and change is growth." It takes a certain type of strength to acknowledge and embrace the types of change that we are compelled to make. Suzanne has found that courage.

My name is Tiffany James, and I am the founder of UndercoverWear, a lingerie home party plan company. In today's climate of all types of in-home sales, a lingerie company seems quite modest and certainly not controversial. However, when I started the company in 1977, boy did I make my mark! At the time, the front-runner in this genre was Tupperware – you know, women "burping" (removing air from) bowls in the living room while their hostess served coffee and sweets to the guests.

Instead, I brought an array of lingerie, including "naughty little nighties", into the home, created a sensuality test to determine how sensual you were, or were not, and encouraged my hostesses to serve wine and cheese. I showed lingerie, corsets, and even my Goody Bag (the name given to the tote bag where the sexiest items were kept hidden until they were revealed) featuring peek-a-boo undies. Based on the response to every party I did, I knew my concept was a winner.

To build my business, I contacted some of the local newspapers about my after-hours activities and received a two-page, full-color spread of one of my UndercoverWear shows in *The Boston Globe.* Suffice it to say, from that moment on, life as I knew it changed.

The free press that I had initiated continued. UndercoverWear was featured in magazines, newspapers, and on a plethora of talk shows, including *Montel Williams*, *Phil Donahue,* and *Oprah*. In fact, *Playboy Magazine* stated that UndercoverWear was an integral part of the sexual revolution of the '80s, although frankly, that had not been my goal – I had done my first show merely to make a little extra money.

The results from all this press were amazing. In five short years, UndercoverWear had sales of over $30,000,000. And sales continued to grow meteorically up to $85,000,000.

My role and honor was to chat with, listen to, and mentor our thousands of independent sales consultants, who we called "UndercoverWear Agents". It was during this time that I was fortunate to meet Suzanne Young. I didn't know about her struggles in her teens and early twenties. When I met her, she was "happily" married and had four young children. I found Suzanne bright, warm, friendly, and engaging. Her husband, on the other hand, was pompous and tended to be charming to every woman other than Suzanne. Suffice it to say, George was not my favorite person. But Suzanne loved him, so that was all that mattered.

In the mid '80s, I held a meeting in Detroit where Suzanne was living. After the meeting, as she was dropping me off at the hotel, Suzanne started talking about her life, her dreams, her aspirations, and her disappointments. No, she didn't "tell all", but for the first time it was clear to me that she did not have a "fairy-tale" marriage. Later, when Suzanne finally had the courage to divorce George, I was secretly delighted. Now it would be her turn to move on and find happiness.

Wrong.

From George, she moved on to Jason. Well, George was a saint compared to Jason. If possible, Jason was even more pompous, egotistical, and condescending. It seemed once again that Suzanne had chosen poorly, but

Jason seemed to make her happy. Of course, I, and many others, often wondered "Why?"

I remember, almost verbatim, the conversation when Suzanne called me to share with me that she was divorcing Jason. She said, "I know you're all going to be so disappointed because you all love Jason so much." Truth be known, we all truly DISLIKED Jason and tolerated him only because we loved Suzanne.

Once again, I wondered how Suzanne could continually make the wrong decisions about men. Why would a vibrant, intelligent woman continue to accept relationships that were not rewarding? Why could Suzanne only find temporary happiness with men that were abusive? I had no answers – only Suzanne could discover the truth.

The answers to these questions, and so many more, lie in this book. You will understand Suzanne's insecurities, and you will relate to her feelings of inadequacy, self-doubt, and poor self-image. Let's face it, at different points in our lives, we have all experienced those same feelings.

The world may have looked at Suzanne with admiration and respect. But Suzanne wasn't ready to embrace life until she began to admire and respect herself in the same way. At the time in her life when she began to love herself unconditionally, she met Kevin. In 2007, they discovered the basic principles of the Law of Attraction and began to study and practice it together. With the knowledge she gained, Suzanne courageously moved forward, and now she's living the life that she'd always secretly desired.

While this book is about Suzanne's life – her struggles and her triumphs – in reality, it is about every woman I know. The best part of *Stepping Into a Life of Joy* is when Suzanne realizes that, "It's not my job to try endless ways to make everyone *else* happy, it's my job to *be* happy!" I just LOVE that.

I applaud Suzanne for opening her heart and soul for all of us to share. I thank her for reminding us that we all deserve happiness and for helping us realize that only *we* can make that happen!

Tiffany James, CEO, UndercoverWear Inc.

Preface

I wanted to write a book that inspires you to reach for the stars and one that helps you realize you have power beyond your wildest imagination to control your life experiences. This power involves a universal law, based on energy, called the Law of Attraction. When you begin to understand how to use it, as I have, it will allow you to attract to yourself a life of love, stability, clarity, happiness, and abundance of all kinds.

When I finally understood how powerful my thoughts were, I began to understand why my life had unfolded the way it did. Throughout this book, I'll be sharing my story along with some ***Law of Attraction principles*** that I've come to realize, influenced the various experiences of my life. Not only did this understanding help me learn to forgive myself and others, it also helped me to realize that, as I practiced managing my own vibration, I had control over my future. This brought me tremendous peace of mind and faith that my happiness was always in my hands.

Law of Attraction Principle

The Law of Attraction is a naturally occurring law in the universe which states that energy of identical vibrational frequencies always coalesces or comes together. *Simply stated, like energy attracts like energy.* According to physics, everything is energy, including our thoughts and therefore this energy becomes attractive in nature.

Each thought produces a different frequency which ranges from low to high depending on the thought. In general, the thoughts that produce bad-feeling emotions vibrate at lower frequencies and those that produce good-feeling emotions vibrate at higher frequencies. As a result, our emotions are letting us know what we can expect to attract, or more accurately how the things we attract will feel when they arrive. Bad feelings attract bad feeling results and good feelings attract good feeling results.

Highest	Joy, Love, Appreciation
↑↑	Happy, Hopeful, Eager
↑↑	Frustration, Overwhelm
↑↑	Worry, Doubt, Blame
↑↑	Anger, Rage, Jealousy
Lowest	Guilt, Fear, Unworthy, Depressed, Powerless

Table 1 - Scale of your emotions

Did you ever have a person pop into your mind and felt it would be fun to connect with them? Maybe it was someone in your current life, or maybe it was a person you knew in the past. It felt so good to think about them that it even made you smile. Suddenly, the phone rang and much to your surprise, the caller was the very person you had been thinking about. This was not a coincidence but an example of The Law of Attraction in action.

You were feeling good and emitting high-frequency energy as you thought about the person you wanted to connect with. That person matched your high-frequency vibrational state and received the impulse to call. The Law of Attraction brought the two of you together via a phone call. In this way, the Law of Attraction can also be thought of as the Law of Rendezvous, because this wasn't just a coincidence – it was an energetic connection.

Law of Attraction Principle

When things rendezvous, they come together. Some people look at the Law of Rendezvous as Divine timing, because it's not an appointment we specifically organize but rather something that the Law of Attraction facilitates, without any planning or effort on our part. These unexpected rendezvous are often called synchronicities or coincidences by people unfamiliar with the Law of Attraction. The truth is, we're constantly being sent a stream of intuitive impulses that guide us toward the energetic thoughts and experiences that match the vibration we're emitting out into the universe. If we're feeling good, we'll rendezvous with good feeling things, people, places, etc. The same holds true for not-so-good feelings.

Please note that I am not writing this book to provide proof that the Law of Attraction exists. You must prove it to yourself. The best way to do this is through your own life experience. Having faith in the unseen and allowing yourself time to practice what you've learned is the best way to begin. To empower yourself and learn more, an expanded explanation about the Law of Attraction itself can be found near the end of the book under *The Law of Attraction in a Nutshell.*

Many of us have learned to work hard, tolerate unhappiness, and push through stress. We've been taught that we need to go through painful experiences before we can be happy. Some of us even postpone the idea of being happy until retirement arrives, only to find out that it doesn't bring happiness either. We struggle with relationships at work and at home, and we repeat the same miserable experiences over and over again. Each year may bring us different and new circumstances, yet our struggles continue because of well-established habits.

The good news is that we never have to settle for less, push through anything, or tolerate the unacceptable to be happy.

Life constantly presents us with options and choices. What we decide to do with them is ultimately up to us. What determines our path in life is how we perceive situations and what we subsequently think. Whether we realize it or not, our thoughts are laying the foundation for our life experiences. If the foundation starts to crumble, we simply need to pick new, supportive thoughts.

Isn't it wonderful that we have the freedom to choose for ourselves?

At the age of 71, I have the freedom of knowing that I will never have to repeat my painful experiences again. There will certainly be emotional ups and downs, but there are no pre-assigned painful lessons that we must learn in order to be happy.

Stepping Into a Life of Joy is the story of my journey of learning to love myself unconditionally and becoming happy from the inside out. It is also about freedom: freedom to be who you are and freedom from worrying about what other people think. I accomplished these things by recognizing old thought patterns and beliefs that didn't serve me and selecting new ones that resonated with me. When we change the quality of our thoughts, we change the quality of our lives. By deciding to choose new thoughts on purpose, I empowered myself, which set me free.

As a self-help seeker all my life, I started reading books to try to answer my big questions about life, such as:

- Why are some people happy while others are miserable?
- Why are some people sick while others are well?
- Why are some people born physically or mentally challenged?
- Why are some people successful while others are not?
- Why are some people rich while others are poor?
- Why are some families so full of anger while others are loving and peaceful?
- Why do bad things happen to good people?

My search for these answers seemed endless, but it led me down a personal path of self-discovery that, by the time I was 57, had become so painful that I knew something needed to change. I didn't know *what* that thing was, but I knew I wanted to find out.

At that time in my life, I had a very good friend and mentor named Katie. For ten years, she had always been very supportive during my times of need. She was full of wisdom, and her guidance for me was invaluable. She became a great help during my struggle through this painful journey, and eventually, she introduced me to the Law of Attraction, for which I will be forever grateful.

Before I was introduced to the Law of Attraction, I could never understand how I'd had the miserable luck of marrying not just one, but two, alcoholic and verbally abusive men. After all the self-help books I'd read, learning about the Law of Attraction was the final missing piece that enabled me to move forward in my life.

I have now been married for ten years to my ideal partner Kevin, a man whom I had thought would be impossible to find. He showed up without any effort on my part and our life together is full of love, understanding, and respect for each other.

How I managed to get through the painful experience of my second divorce and came to enjoy the happy, successful, and rewarding life I now have is what eventually inspired me to write this book.

Some of the names in my story have been changed for the privacy of the people involved. I know that we all do the best we can with the knowledge we have at the time of each life-changing event, so I don't blame anyone for the painful moments in my life. Instead, I hope I can help others to see, as I have, how each of us is accountable for our own life journeys. Defining moments can be viewed as failures or successes. We can take on the role of victim or become the victor. The thoughts we choose at these times make the difference as to whether we get stuck in a rut or move on. *Stepping Into a Life of Joy* is about moving forward!

Prologue: Shocked

In the early morning of January 2004, I was on my way to work to the company that my husband Jason and I owned together. The driving was difficult as there was a cold wet drizzle of snow and rain steadily falling. The roads were slippery, and the dividing lines were very difficult to see. Little did I know that within the next 30 minutes my life would change forever.

I was listening to the news and was worried that the road conditions might make me late. This made me nervous because I knew how mad Jason would get when anyone arrived late. Luckily, I got to work just in time to avoid being yelled at. I ran in and heard the phone ringing and wondered why Jason had not picked it up. I saw Jason in his office with the door closed.

I pick up the phone in the showroom. I said hello. An unknown male voice answered and proceeded to tell me that my husband had been having an affair with a young girl, a barmaid that I knew, and that he'd purchased a house for her to live in. He offered to provide proof if I wanted it. I didn't learn all the sordid details until later, but this was enough to shock me.

In all honesty, most of my life I'd practiced pretending that *nothing bothered me* so, even though I had a huge knot in my stomach, I didn't have to struggle too hard to hold my emotions back. I decided that before I said anything to Jason, I knew I needed more proof, plus I didn't want to cause a big scene in front of our employees.

My secretary and I had been friends for twenty years and we confided everything to each other. After Jason left the office, I told her about the phone call. To my amazement, she didn't even seem shocked and the first comment she made was, "I've been dropping hints to you for months, but you didn't seem to hear what I've been saying." She'd suspected he was having an affair for a while. She kept quiet because she didn't want to interfere with our marriage and she was worried that her job would be at stake. Yes, she had dropped hints to me, but I must admit I'd been living in denial.

I took a couple of hours off from work to do some investigating of the details I'd been given. That evening, as I left work with the information I had learned, I felt devastated. When I got home, I fell to my knees sobbing. This was my second marriage and once again it was obviously going to end in divorce. At age 57, I felt like a total failure: very old, alone, and powerless. I cried out for someone – anyone – to please help me to get through this! My wonderful, devoted dog Roxie ran to me and licked the tears that were streaming down my face. Thank God for dogs as her unconditional love for me was always there. At that moment, I took a deep breath and was thankful that, through thick and thin, Roxie had always been by my side. Her unwavering love brought me a moment of relief and I said out loud "someone please help me!"

Days and weeks of pain continued as I began to uncover the facts. My husband had taken part of our retirement money, bought a house behind my back, and had his girlfriend and her two little kids living in it. This had been going on for nine months.

During the seventeen years I'd known him and the seven years we'd been married, his drinking had increased. At this point in our lives, he was in an argumentative mood most of the time and usually smelled of booze. He was leading a double life, and I'd become so good at living in denial that he'd gotten away with it until that fateful phone call.

PART ONE:

Role Models

Comfort Zones

Have you ever wondered why we, as human beings, are so hard on ourselves? Why is it that we can be true, loving, and loyal friends to others, but we cannot do the same for ourselves? Why is it that we judge ourselves so easily? We freely accept, support, and encourage others but we often discount our own feelings and desires.

We don't even realize that we're making ourselves unhappy by ignoring our feelings, wants, or needs. This way of living becomes an *uncomfortable comfort zone.*

Looking back on my life, I'm now aware that the most painful times in my life were a direct result of me becoming my own worst enemy and letting my mind consistently wander into self-criticism and self-doubt. I had developed a habit of ignoring my feelings and became used to negative self-talk and the feeling of unworthiness. As my habit grew it became easier to love and support others than to care about me or be honest with myself.

In hindsight, it's now clear that worrying about what other people think attracts disaster. When it comes to the Law of Attraction the opinion of yourself far outweighs the opinion of others, but we are trained from birth to listen to our parent's opinion on everything. When I was told to be quiet, I did. When I was told to sit down, I did, and on and on it went.

This is how I began to believe that happiness came from pleasing others. I believed that I wasn't good enough to be loved unless I met the endless expectations other people wanted from me. Over my lifetime, I became quite good at crushing my own spirit and settling for less. So how did I learn to live in an uncomfortable comfort zone? Here's how it started for me.

I was born on a cold winter morning in the small town of Yale, MI. I arrived on March 9, 1947, a healthy, chubby baby weighing in at around eight pounds. It immediately made my parents very happy to see how healthy I was. My mom told many stories of how I was born a happy baby – and for me, oh how wonderful it was to be welcomed into the loving, open, and accepting arms of my parents! I was blessed from the start.

My mother was Theresa Rohrer, an attractive young woman who was twenty-six years old when I was born. She had beautiful blue eyes and blonde hair and even after having given birth to my older sister Linda and me, still had a gorgeous shape that I imagine many women envied. She'd been a model before we kids were born, known for her shapely gorgeous legs which had earned her the title "Miss Legs of Chicago". She modeled for many companies, including Coca-Cola, and was featured on large billboards along the sides of the roads in Michigan. As a small child, I was always happy to see her smiling face on those billboards, holding the well-known 1940s glass bottle of Coke to her lips.

She had a heart of gold and loved flowers, animals, and all of nature. Not only was she an attractive model, she was also valedictorian of her high school. She loved gardening in the summer and painting during the long Michigan winters. Oil painting was her favorite and when she painted scenes of wildlife and nature, they looked stunningly realistic. She also had a rare gift and ability when it came to painting portraits. Not only did the finished product always resemble the person to a tee, the sparkling eyes became uncannily alive. People often wanted to pay her for her work, but she was true to herself and chose to avoid the stress of having to produce paintings for money and wisely kept it as a hobby throughout her life.

My dad, John Rohrer, was born premature on September 9, 1919. His mother, Margaret, had already had several miscarriages before his birth so naturally she was very worried about her tiny newborn child surviving. Grandpa was often out of work and times were so difficult that, after my dad's birth, they didn't have enough money to heat their home. I'll never forget my grandma telling me a story of how worried she was about her tiny premature baby surviving throughout the cold autumn, so she kept "little John" warm by putting him in the oven! In the end, my grandma deeply cherished my dad as he became their only surviving child.

I remember grandma telling me the story of how her faith in God kept her going through the sadness of losing her children and the hard times they lived through with very little money. I really didn't know what she meant by *faith,* but I thought it was amazing that whatever this thing called *faith* was, it had kept her strong during many difficult times. It had even inspired her to come up with the idea of keeping my dad warm and alive in the oven!

My dad was a very talented and handsome man. He loved music, and at an early age he helped his mom earn a little extra money by entertaining people. She played the piano and he accompanied her on his drums. Every dime they made helped the family survive. He was considered a child prodigy when it came to his skill on the drums. When he was only five, he was invited to share his talent by playing his drums in John Philip Sousa's band which was performing in my dad's hometown of Detroit while on tour.

My dad was a great storyteller. (Maybe he's inspiring me to tell my own story!) He loved telling us about his time in the army during World War II. Countless interesting and entertaining stories grew out of his wartime experiences. One of his favorite stories was about how he avoided actual combat overseas because he had the pleasure of playing drums in a band organized to entertain troops stationed in the United States. He always appreciated that he'd been given that opportunity and never had to risk his life fighting, unlike many of his male friends.

I am so happy and grateful that I was born into my parents' warm and loving home. They were a beautiful couple and loved each other very much. They were admired and respected and they were great role models, full of love for each other and for their three girls. They valued close, warm family time together. Every summer we spent several weeks vacationing at Houghton Lake in central Michigan with extended family, including our grandparents and sometimes our aunt, as well as our girlfriends. Throughout our lives we ate dinner together, sitting around the table every evening and discussing how our day had gone. Our parents also made sure we had plenty of visiting time with our grandparents on both sides of the family during the holidays and on our birthdays. It was a joy to be a part of such a close-knit, loving family. They had many friends and made sure to set aside time for fun with them, which included bridge clubs, evening parties, golfing, and boating. They loved animals, so we enjoyed having many dogs and cats. They showed and shared love easily and even though we had some difficult times as all families do, we had lots of smiles and hugs along the way.

A couple of years after I was born, my parents, my older sister Linda, and I moved from the small northern Michigan town of Yale to Grosse Ile, a small island in Michigan in the middle of the Detroit River. Because it is only five miles wide by ten miles long, one way or another, everybody knew everybody. At the beginning of my life on the island, my dad, loving music as he did, was a band teacher. Within a few years, he became the principal of Grosse Ile Elementary School, the only public elementary school on the island.

Habits

A *habit* is something that a person does in a regular and repeated way. The families we are born into have many habits which are passed along from generation to generation. Sometimes they're passed on to us on purpose and sometimes they're given to us by default, simply because our parents or caregivers don't know any different.

As babies, before language skills develop, we communicate with others by expressing our emotions. Thus, we begin to learn early on whether we can trust our emotions. Babies need comfort and attention when they're hungry, have a wet diaper, don't feel good, or want to be held. Showing our emotions is the only way we can communicate to anyone as an infant, so we cry, or coo, or smile accordingly. Trusting that our emotions are valid begins at birth and trusting others that they will respond to our needs begins at this time too. It's easy to see how habits of trusting or not trusting in others and in learning if we can trust our own emotional guidance develops from birth and throughout our early years.

As we begin to grow up, these habits or patterns of behavior attract circumstances that may not reflect *our* true desires because they were either picked up during infancy or passed along to us by someone else. As a result, these inherited or acquired habits can often stir up unrest or even anxiety within us as we become older and more independent.

Since being fed is associated with comfort and love, my food habits started as an infant. My mom used to tell me how she struggled to get my older sister to eat and felt guilty because my sister was considered underweight according to doctors' standards at that time. When I came along, she was thrilled with how much I loved my bottle, so she fed me as much as I wanted (even to the point that my stomach was so full I'd just simply throw up). Because of this, I began associating the feeling of a full stomach with the feeling of being held and loved by my mom. This helps me understand why, as I became older, I'd turned to food until I felt stuffed to comfort myself during times of stress. Other people may learn the habit of overeating because that is what they saw their parents and other family members do. It doesn't really matter how any of us acquire dysfunctional eating habits. What does matter is that none of us do this to ourselves on purpose. It is a learned behavior, and habits can be changed once we truly decide we want to begin new self-supportive ways of thinking about food.

Law of Attraction Principle

A habit is a learned behavior. Once we are aware that we have a habit that no longer serves us, it then becomes a choice. It's important to understand that the Law of Attraction will support our habit, whether it serves us or not. This is why people say it takes 30 days to make or break a habit because over time, as momentum builds up, the power behind the Law of Attraction strengthens and it continues to bring us more thoughts with the same vibrational essence of the habit you are building or breaking.

Beliefs

As babies, we have feelings based on what's going on inside our bodies and from the energy, or vibration, coming from the environment that surrounds us each day. The energy from the words we hear spoken by the people around us, including the tone of voice and bodily gestures immediately begin to affect us.

> ***Law of Attraction Principle***
>
> A belief is only a thought that we think over and over again. This thought may come from others, or it may originate from our own experience. A belief is not true or false, good or bad, or right or wrong. Beliefs exist because we have been continually thinking about things in a certain way and thus attracting experiences equal to our habits of thought. As a result, we assume that our beliefs must be true because we keep attracting more of what we are thinking about. The good news is that all the beliefs we have acquired in childhood, which no longer resonate with us, can be changed by choosing new thoughts.

At the age of three or so, after my younger sister was born, I remember overhearing other adults say to my parents during the parties they used to have, "Oh, you had another girl. I bet you were wishing for a boy!" We all know that "fathers hope to have a boy to follow in their footsteps and carry on the family name." Although I may have been too young to understand the discussion I'd overheard, I could feel the worrisome energy in the room. My belief that boys were more valuable than girls innocently began at this young age. Of course, my parents were happy to have three girls, but I believed that they probably would have rather had a boy because of what I'd listened to that night.

Being a middle child, I wasn't getting much attention after my younger sister was born. Since I didn't want my dad to be disappointed in only having girls, I began wishing I was a boy, so I could make him happier with me than my sisters. I even went as far as trying to stand at the toilet to pee as I'd seen my dad do. Of course, after several attempts, I quickly found out this was pretty messy. It never worked out!

I was naturally athletic, and all sports came easily to me. Outdoors was one of my favorite places to be. I loved playing ball with my dad and as I got older, I was the one who was willing to help him out with chores like mowing the lawn or shoveling snow. I became the tomboy of the family in the false belief that if I acted like a boy, I would be the favorite child.

Law of Attraction Principle

The Law of Attraction lines up experiences that match the vibrational energy of our thoughts and resulting beliefs. They can support us or hold us back during our life. Continuing in a belief system that doesn't resonate with us is a choice. Choosing our thoughts wisely can help us change our life from bad to good, and from good to great!

The Art of People-Pleasing

What is people-pleasing? I think many of us, as children, were trained to do what the adults in our lives asked or demanded of us. Adults have expected us to do these things, so they could be happy, and children complied to avoid punishment for not doing what they were told. I developed a belief that it was my job to do things to make other people happy and if I did, not only would I be considered a *good* girl I thought it would make me lovable.

It amazes me how young we are when we start developing thoughts that don't really serve us. For example, I began realizing as a toddler that when my dad was sitting in his lazy-boy chair it meant it was time for me (and my sisters) to be quiet and let him rest or he would become ornery. By the time I was five, I had already learned that I was a *good* girl if I cleaned my plate at dinner time. I learned that when I did what my parents asked of me it made them happy and it also made me (inaccurately) tie my self-worth to the need to have to do things for others first in order to be worthy of receiving love and respect. This is how my habit of people-pleasing began, although I didn't understand the concept at such a young age.

Law of Attraction Principle

When we're trained to do things or behave in a certain way to make other people happy, we lose our ability to listen to, and follow, our own inner guidance. It's also dis-empowering to the one expecting us to appease or change for them as they begin to think that happiness only comes when other people do things for them. This becomes a no-win situation for everyone because neither is learning how to listen to their emotions, trust their own inner guidance, and learn how to become the creator of their own happiness.

Another dis-empowering habit I developed at a very young age was the habit of worrying about what other people thought. Once we begin this habit, we often unknowingly sabotage ourselves. When I was in first grade, my favorite time of the day was recess. Our elementary school didn't have air-conditioning and on one unusually hot, spring day, I was extra-eager to get outside for recess to cool off. When the bell rang, I quickly ran to my favorite playground equipment called the Maypoles. It was a tall, sturdy pole with six long, strong, reinforced wires coming from the top of it, each with a set of handlebars on the end. I grabbed the first one, and soon all the spots were filled with kids who were eager to run 'round and round'. Those of us who loved the Maypoles knew that the faster we ran, the higher we flew off the ground. We burned up lots of energy and had so much fun. I always had dreams of flying as a little kid and that was what it felt like to me when we were going really fast. It produced a great feeling of freedom and what kid doesn't appreciate that feeling?

On this particular hot day, as I was up high in the air, my hands began sweating. A few minutes into the joy of feeling free and flying, I began to lose my grip and *kabang*! I flew off the Maypoles onto the ground with a big thud. A teacher came running over to me and asked if I was okay. Even though my right arm was killing me, I lied and said I was fine. She offered to take me into the principal's office for help, but I refused. I pretended I was okay. My thought, at the age of five and a half, was that only bad kids were sent to the principal's office and I knew I didn't want to be thought of as a bad kid. But, even more importantly, I didn't want to go the principal's office because my dad was the principal! I *believed* that I would embarrass myself and disappoint my dad. This experience of purposefully choosing to act in a certain way to please others, even though the choice didn't feel good to me, contributed to the belief that I could not be my authentic self in front of others.

I finished out the school day never crying and pretending it didn't hurt. I kept telling myself that "everything would be fine." Luckily, I'd often heard my mother say those exact words to comfort me or my sisters and even my dad during difficult times. As I silently repeated it to myself that day, it was like magic, and it gave me the strength to accept the pain until I could go home.

Law of Attraction Principle

When we are going through a painful time, physically or mentally, finding a way to temporarily feel better will help us in the moment. By choosing thoughts that comfort us our energy rises and our pain eases up. This is a form of distraction and it's how I was able to get through many hours in school despite the pain of my broken arm. Distraction doesn't help us get to the root of the problem of why we attracted the pain in the first place, thus it isn't a long-term solution to attracting a pain free life, however, as a young child or anyone who's searching for some quick relief, the Law of Attraction can support us in this way. It's a good starting point as it changes our energy field and helps us move forward, one step at a time, through any painful *now moments* we may experience.

When I got home, I immediately ran to my mother crying. I had suppressed it all day long until I was in the comfort of her arms. I showed her my swollen, bruised arm. She quickly took me to the doctor and sure enough, the X-rays showed that I'd broken my arm just above the wrist. After the cast was put on, the pain immediately eased up.

Our parents are our role models. To this day, I appreciate that I learned how to support myself by thinking optimistically during painful times like my mom always did. In fact, that eventful day had a huge impact on me. From that point on, no matter how painful or embarrassing something might have seemed, I temporarily got through it much more easily by thinking all the comforting thoughts that my mother had taught me.

My dad was well-known as the principal of the school where all the parents on Grosse Ile sent their children. Attending church each week was positively viewed by everyone in the small island community. As a result, after my dad became the principal of the school, our family began going to church.

It always felt to me that we were attending church for the social aspect and for the sake of appearances only. Grandma Rohrer was a strict churchgoer and I saw her pray a lot, but our parents never taught us any prayers. I never heard them discuss why we needed to go to church and I never felt that any of us particularly enjoyed going to church. We girls were each baptized in a Methodist Church in Detroit. My dad's mother was actively involved with that church, so I assumed that we were baptized there to make my grandma happy. Obviously, the art of people pleasing didn't just begin with me! As you can see, it's easily handed down from generation to generation.

I remember Sunday mornings very well. We had one small bathroom that we all shared, and it was often busy and stressful for my mother as she was the one who got us 3 girls cleaned up and ready to go. She would patiently brush our hair – not an easy task with three girls – and helped us put on our dresses which seemed like a requirement to attend church. Because the salary that my dad received as a principle, we couldn't afford to buy clothes from the store. As such, my mom sewed our Sunday dresses so that we would fit into the church community. I secretly wished that we could go to the store and buy prettier dresses so I could look like the other girls but this never happened.

Eventually, I began to resent having to go to church but decided not to complain or voice my opinion. I worried that if I said I didn't want to go, I would disappoint my parents. My people-pleasing habit had become so strong that speaking my truth didn't even seem like an option.

Self-Sabotage

Going from fourth into fifth grade was a difficult time for me. I was becoming very self-conscious about my maturing body as I started developing breasts way ahead of my older sister and my girlfriends. In addition to having what I considered big boobs, I was overweight. In fifth grade, I weighed 120 pounds. My mom, dad, and sisters were all thin. I remember weighing more than my mom at the age of ten and feeling so horrible about it. I often felt embarrassed as I looked in the mirror and would subject myself to strong, but silent, inner self-criticism. I covered up my developing body with big baggy sweatshirts and often felt uglier and fatter than my skinny, bony, flat-chested girlfriends.

I disliked the way I looked so much that I hated going to gym class. When I ran back and forth in the gymnasium for the various activities we were required to do, my boobs flopped up and down, and I was totally embarrassed. It became such a dilemma for me that I came up with an ideal solution – or so I thought!

During that era, *Leave it to Beaver* was a popular TV show. My mom had plenty of shirtwaist dresses like the TV mom, Mrs. Cleaver, which came with a wide elastic belt to make them look attractive. This belt would come in handy for me. In 1957, there were no handy stretch sports bras with racerbacks or even small beginner bras for young girls who were just developing, and boy, as a result I *almost* invented one!

How? Well, one day I took one of my mom's wide elastic belts out of her closet and stretched it around my chest. I put my undershirt and my big baggy sweatshirt on and *voila*, my boobs were held down and supported, and I was finally flat-chested like all the girls in my gym class. What a great feeling! I loved many of the things we did in gym class, yet I denied myself the feeling of joy I could have experienced because I hated how embarrassed I felt when I ran. On that day, I had a very brief glimpse of what it felt like to be happy and *free to be me*. What fun it was to fully enjoy the gym class!

Unfortunately, it backfired on me. After about fifteen minutes of running around, the belt started slipping down. First, one boob popped out. I saw what was happening, and I was shocked to realize that others could also see this weird sight. Then, the other popped out, and I was back to the feeling of total embarrassment! I thought I would never get over it. Lo and behold, I had one more childhood-defining moment that took my self-esteem to an even lower level.

Hating Myself

Growing up on an island with water everywhere, my parents made sure that we learned to swim at a young age. We were allowed to walk to our friends' homes all over the south end of the island to play. There were small creeks and bridges to cross and the big Detroit River was within arm's reach. In 1958, we joined a country club (the inexpensive one, since we couldn't afford the ritzy one) which had an unheated outdoor pool where we could learn to swim.

I loved water from the very beginning and still do to this day. I quickly learned how to hold my breath, dive down, and allow myself to float up. Being submerged under the water all by myself where everything was quiet and peaceful gave me an amazing feeling of happiness. As a chubby little girl, I found it very easy to float. When I tipped my head far back, submerging my eyes and leaving my nose out of the water just enough to get air, my fat little belly kept me afloat easily. I saw how hard it was for some kids to learn how to float and swim, so I must admit I felt quite proud of myself for accomplishing this so easily.

When I started developing a female shape, I became very self-conscious wearing a bathing suit. Besides being fat, my boobs weren't hidden like they were in a baggy sweatshirt and I felt very self-conscious and embarrassed about anyone seeing my shapely body.

Law of Attraction Principle

The Law of Attraction is always working whether we know it or not. As such, when we enter into an experience and are *not feeling good* about ourselves, we will always attract a *not-good-feeling* experience as a result.

Keep in mind that swimsuits were very different in 1958. My swimsuit was an ordinary tank top style, cotton blend, one-piece suit. It didn't have crisscross straps like the racerback styles of today, which hold the bathing suit on securely while diving and swimming and this was about to play out in a most unexpected and unpleasant way!

I was good at all the various swim styles that we were taught – the butterfly, breaststroke, sidestroke, and backstroke – so I joined the swim team. I was a confident swimmer, so I enjoyed competing against others. When I was ten, I participated on a relay team at a swim meet where all the parents and other family members were eagerly watching and cheering us on. There were moms, dads, brothers, and sisters, and it was exciting because my team was winning.

I was assigned to swim the backstroke during the last leg of the race. I was happy to be in this position and was enthusiastic as I entered the water. I was a strong backstroke swimmer and I knew deep down inside that my team could count on me. I jumped in and began focusing on arriving at the finish line before my competitor. My pace was fast and deliberate, and I was in the lead after 3 laps had gone by. Suddenly and unexpectedly, one of my shoulder straps slipped off, followed shortly afterward by the other. It only took a couple of seconds for me to realize that I was nude from the waist up as I approached the last lap. How quickly my mind went from wanting my team to win to self-preservation! I felt horrible! All the spectators, including the men and the boys, had seen my boobs! I stopped and pulled up my bathing suit and continued swimming.

At that point, we'd lost the race as I was too far behind to catch up. Not only was I totally embarrassed, I also felt very guilty for stopping in the middle of the event to pull up my suit. Yes, I listened to my gut instinct and I chose to pull my bathing suit up because it felt like the right thing to do for me but the defining moment for me was the total humiliation I felt because everyone had seen my boobs! I learned at that moment to devalue the benefit of listening to my gut instinct because I focused too much on the idea of letting my team down and on my negative self-talk about the others seeing me naked from the waist up. This is an example of how I began to teach myself to ignore my intuition and my true gut feelings.

Law of Attraction Principle

Our intuition, gut instinct, or our *inner being*, is always speaking to us and trying to guide us along our path in life. When we pay attention to our gut instinct within the first 1-3 seconds (within seconds I knew I had to stop and pull my suit up) and make decisions based on the feelings we are having, we will make decisions that are right for us. If it feels bad, say no. When it feels good, say yes.

Sometime during fifth grade, my mom must have noticed how unhappy I was with myself and she took me to the doctor for a checkup. Not only did she worry about me being unhappy she was also concerned that I was overweight for my age. As a model, my mother had learned from her own experience that good looks and physical appearance were of utmost importance. A woman with those attributes went a long way in the very male-oriented world of the 1950s. When I got older, I could feel her worry and concern about me being fat, unhappy, and lonely, and I'm sure the doctor did too. He told her it was time for me to go on a diet and gave my mother instructions on what to serve me so that I could lose some weight. I didn't know what to expect as I'd never heard of such a thing as a diet.

Back in those days, my mom fried everything in leftover bacon grease that she saved in a can. I loved her cooking, especially when she coated chicken pieces in eggs and flour and fried them in the bacon grease. I loved the mashed potatoes with gravy and the fried potatoes (yes – in bacon grease) that she regularly gave us with many of our dinners. She also made excellent chicken with dumplings and gravy. With every dinner, we had a wonderful dessert to enjoy if we finished our first course. My sisters didn't care about finishing their first course, but you better believe I loved cleaning my plate, so I could have dessert. We also got to have a snack of some sort before going to bed, like buttered popcorn or ice cream with Sander's Hot Fudge chocolate topping poured all over it. That way of eating, which might be considered unhealthy today, didn't seem to affect my sisters, my dad, or my mom; I was the only one who easily gained weight. Of course, the truth is that I was the only one who loved big portions and wanted second helpings too!

When my diet started, I began to feel deprived and different from everyone else in my family. I could no longer drink whole milk like the others – only skim milk for me – and I couldn't have butter on my potatoes or vegetables. My mom carefully followed whatever else the doctor had told her to do regarding what I ate. Of course, there were no more second helpings for me, or desserts, or snacks, so I began to sneak cookies when no one was looking. I went to the depths of sneakiness during this diet. At one point, I decided to steal a candy bar from the one and only local drugstore on the island. I was caught in the act and denied that I'd done it. The owner, who had caught me, knew I was the principal's daughter. I think he didn't force me to confess out of respect for my dad. I felt tremendous relief when he didn't make me empty my pockets (where I'd hidden the candy bar) and that he didn't turn me in. I learned how horrible I felt when I lied to someone else and never wanted to risk having that feeling of shame inside of me again. I can't even remember if I ate the candy bar!

In hindsight, I appreciate that my mother cared enough to help me become physically healthier. By the time I entered sixth grade, I'd lost twenty pounds and my mom was very happy to see her fat little girl blossoming into a beautiful young lady. I felt better seeing my mom not worried about me being fat anymore, but I was even more self-conscious about my shapely body. Of course, I didn't feel like the beautiful young lady she thought I'd become. By this time, I had developed a very strong pattern of negative self-talk when I looked in the mirror. Big baggy sweatshirts were still my favorite attire and even on hot days, I would rather sweat and be covered up than show my maturing body. During that era, the only bras that would fit someone my size were hard cotton, pointy, Madonna-style bras, and that just made things worse for me. So, when the time came that I started becoming interested in boys, I was far, far away from thinking that any boy would ever be interested in me and find me attractive.

Boys: The Unknown

Since I had no brothers, I was always curious about what boys might look like without their clothes on. I had occasionally briefly seen my dad naked (always by mistake of course) but this had only made me even more curious. I remember my older sister and I coaxing a young neighbor boy aged four or so into our garage and asking him to pull his pants down. This how we first saw what a little boy's penis looked like.

As a teen, I liked the idea of babysitting to make some money and I slowly started getting jobs babysitting for other families on the island. The first time I had to change a baby boy's diaper was when I learned a little more about boys' bodies. I remember it well as I had not been told much about boys' anatomy. From the experience in the garage with my sister and the neighbor boy, I knew they had something different than what girls had and I knew they peed out of this thing we called his pee-pee.

One evening, the parents I was babysitting for had instructed me that if their eight-month-old son woke up, most likely around ten o'clock, it would probably mean that he needed his diaper changed. Like clockwork, he began to cry at the predicted time. I cautiously got him out of his crib and moved him to the changing table. I unpinned his cloth diaper (no handy disposables in those days) and saw that his penis was different than the boy's in the garage. It was stiff and standing straight up. I proceeded to clean him up and shortly afterward, he started to pee. I strapped him in and went to find a new diaper for him. When I returned with the dry diaper his penis was soft and lying down. I was shocked. Thinking I'd broken his penis when I wiped him, I was worried sick. I put the new dry diaper on him and was totally afraid to tell his parents what had happened. So, I didn't. When they returned home, I told them everything had been fine. Since I really thought I'd broken his penis, I carried this guilt for quite some time until I eventually learned more about penises.

PART TWO:

Spreading My Wings

Dating Begins

I didn't date anyone until I fell in love – or at least what I thought was love – with the first boy who wanted to steadily date me when I was fifteen. His name was George, and in hindsight, it certainly wasn't love as I know it today. I thought it was love, which included being attracted to his cool car and the fact that he was a great dancer. He was quite entertaining and easy to talk to and he enjoyed telling lots of jokes. Unlike other high-school kids, he had money to spend because he was two years older than me and out of high school with a well-paid job in a Detroit auto plant. I liked his rebellious nature since I was the opposite and had no courage to speak up about anything. My parents didn't approve of my relationship with him because he was older than me. They had heard through our small island grapevine that he drank and partied often and had grown up in a dysfunctional home. I didn't know what a dysfunctional home was and even though they may have been right, I didn't want to listen to them. They also didn't like the fact that he was Catholic since we went to the Episcopalian church, and some of the island people might frown on this mixing of religions.

All this worry on my parents' part didn't make any sense to me so for the first time in my life, I decided to go against their wishes and become even more involved with George.

They were not happy that I wanted to see him daily after school. At age seventeen, I began to sneak out of my house late in the night to meet up with him in his cool car. Eventually, this led to my first sexual experience.

Learning about Sex

In 1963, there was no formal sex education at our school and certainly no one talked about it with me. I was very naive about sex at this age and when George began to pressure me to have sex with him, I was confused.

I really knew nothing about it except my mom had told me that girls have periods because we have babies and men cannot. They have a penis and girls have a vagina and that was about all I knew. I didn't know the purpose of the penis or the vagina although I'd heard from other girls that the penis could fit into the vagina. I also knew nothing about masturbation or that there could be pleasure during sex, so I really didn't understand why anyone would want a penis in her vagina.

When George was nineteen and I was seventeen, he began telling me that he would get sore "balls" if he got "hard" and couldn't "come" and that it would really be great if he could put his "dick" inside of me and "come" to relieve the pain from his "blue balls", as he called them. (Okay, so I was REALLY innocent and uninformed!)

I certainly wasn't thinking of the possibility of pregnancy at that time and I quickly fell into my people-pleasing role and said "Okay." The truth was that although I might have been curious about the idea, I didn't want his penis in my vagina! He told me that if I really loved him, I would want to do this thing he was asking of me.

So, I lied to myself, played the pretend game and said he could have sex with me. After all, I didn't want to upset him or lose his love which I feared might happen if I refused. I did not enjoy it the first time – it hurt! – and it hurt for many times after that. I was totally unknowledgeable as to what was going on. I didn't know the benefit of using lubrication and I didn't know about orgasms, so I had no clue that anything could ever feel good. We didn't use any protection during sex as this was not talked about at school or in our home either. My mother came to me once in my senior year and offered me birth control pills as she'd begun to suspect that we were progressing to sex. I thought she would be shocked if I told her I'd been having sex for about a year and had never gotten pregnant! So, I lied to her – and to myself, which brought even more shame and guilt – and said I didn't need them and that she had nothing to worry about.

Even though we had sex often, I didn't get pregnant while I was in high school. I thought this was because, as George had told me, his doctor had said that he had such a low sperm count that he couldn't get anyone pregnant. Naively, I believed him, which led me to develop a false belief that pregnancy was not going to happen to me.

Because I wanted to please my parents, I tried hard to get all A's in school. I caused myself a lot of stress with this choice which resulted in many migraine headaches that forced me to go to bed in a dark, quiet room until I recovered. Although the long hours of studying may have taken their toll on me, they did produce the pleasure of my repeatedly making the honor roll. As a result, I received a one-year scholarship to Western Michigan University. In the fall of 1965, I was happily looking forward to going off to college soon.

During this era, women who were in television shows always played a role of stay at home moms. It was obvious our society clearly admired women who were housewives and mothers. My parents were thrilled that I'd earned a scholarship which had relieved them of the burden of paying for my first year at Western. I started thinking about a career and was eager to find a profession that really interested me. I told my mom I wanted to become a psychiatrist but all I remember my mother saying was, "Don't worry about that now, dear – just go and enjoy yourself and find a good man to marry."

George was not going to go to college because he was very happy making lots of money as a millwright in a Detroit auto plant. When he found out that I was going to be leaving him to go off to college in a city that was a three-hour drive from Grosse Ile, he was disappointed and got angry. He had shown signs of jealousy throughout our two years together. He would often yell angry words at me when I went out with my girlfriends and I naively decided he got mad because he loved me so much that he couldn't stand to be without me. I was too young to have learned that people's anger is often a reflection of their own lack of self-worth. I had not noticed that this was his way of always getting what he wanted, from me or anyone else. What I didn't realize then was that he was copying a habit of behavior he'd learned from his parents.

I chose to go to college which meant we wouldn't be dating anymore because Western Michigan University was in Kalamazoo, a 3-hour drive from Grosse Ile. My parents were elated, to say the least, as they thought that my relationship with George was finally ending. They were so proud of me, their "all-A" student who had earned a scholarship. I knew I'd disappointed them by dating George, so I was pleased to see them happy with me for a change.

College

I don't have a lot of vivid memories of my first year at college, probably because it was such a huge adjustment. I spent most of my time studying in my all-girls dorm and nothing very exciting ever happened. I quickly missed the security of home where I had someone who always did my laundry and who fixed all the meals, I would eat every day. At school, there were so many more responsibilities – and unlimited food choices. I could eat as often and as much as I wanted, and I began to find a lot of comfort in eating. It helped me to ignore my new feelings of fear, loneliness, and worry about failing. Of course, I began to gain weight. I didn't pay too much attention to it until I went home for the Christmas break and my Mom mentioned how much heavier I looked compared to when I'd left. I could tell she was worried which made me start worrying, too. The only comfort I found was in knowing that at least I was getting good grades which pleased my parents. That was the one area where I was confident. I had no confidence in my overweight body.

The other disappointment that I was dealing with was the fact that my parents were unhappy that George had suddenly decided he was going to apply to Western Michigan University, so he could keep an eye on me. To his own and everyone else's surprise, he was accepted. Having him there made it almost impossible for me to even think of dating anyone else which was a big disappointment to my mom. I knew her big hopes for me were simply that I get good grades and find a new boyfriend.

That year went by quickly. I experienced some new things, such as racism, for the first time. Growing up on a secluded island, I'd never experienced racism so it had never impacted my life. Seeing people treated differently because of their looks made me feel bad and I tried to avoid discussions that centered on this topic. I hated the idea of discrimination as I knew very well how awful it was to feel different such as being the fat one in an otherwise thin family and to be judged for it. This again confirmed in my mind that I wished everyone could be unconditionally loved and not judged for who they were or how they looked.

I truly enjoyed one class in which I studied five different religions. It really helped me understand how, even though each religion's teachings and rituals are different, all religions are interconnected through their overall spiritual concepts of love and peace. As a result, I decided that I enjoyed being an open-minded and spiritually-oriented person. I found it easy to accept all religions and I liked the idea of people being able to choose which religion they wanted to follow, if any at all. Personally, I embraced the idea of choosing not to follow any specific religion and just be open minded and accepting of all.

Since I spent so much time studying, it was easier to continue seeing George than to try to find a new boyfriend as my mom was hoping. My self-esteem was dropping as I continued to gain weight. My fear of being unattractive made it easy to continue with George because it provided me the security of knowing I had someone to date and go to parties with. I knew he was meeting other women in our first year there, but I didn't say anything to him about us being an exclusive couple for fear he'd leave me. Then, I really would be alone.

At the end of my first year at Western, all my friends were eager to go home for the summer. Like them, I missed my friends, my family, and my dog . . . but unlike them, I was dreading going home again.

Moral Dilemma

A few weeks before I started preparing to go home for the summer, I found out that I was pregnant.

Okay, I did mention that I was very naïve and had believed George when he'd said that his sperm count was too low to get me pregnant! The doctor had confirmed that I was about six weeks along and now our future was quickly changing. I was scared to death to tell my parents because I knew I would really be letting them down. Living on the small island, gossip would spread. I'd be a huge embarrassment to our family.

It took all the courage I could muster to finally tell my parents the bad news and as I'd expected, they were very upset and disappointed in me. After many tears had been shed, all the emotions had come out and the facts had been faced, my parents offered me one of two choices: either I could marry George, or they would be more than happy to pay for an abortion.

Even though abortions were not talked about or even legally available back in 1966, they knew a doctor who would perform one for me. Since my scholarship only covered one year of college, my parents told me that if I chose to get married, they would not pay my future college fees but if I got an abortion, I could continue at Western and they would support me.

Here I was, at nineteen, facing a situation that I knew would change my life forever. Should I get married or get an abortion? I had met George when I was only fifteen. Throughout the years we'd been together, we'd been saying "I love you", so I assumed we were in love – but we'd never talked about marriage.

I felt my parents being critical of me in a way I'd never experienced before. Oh yes, I did feel their judgment around me being "the fat one" in the family. However, with this new experience, I easily recognized that "unconditional" was not a part of their definition of love and that certain conditions had to be met or I would be unacceptable in their eyes. It was a defining moment for me. My urge to know and experience true unconditional love – the same urge I had experienced when I was put on a diet and when I saw discrimination against black students for the first time in college – was stronger than ever.

The thought of an abortion was much worse than the thought of not completing college. It certainly didn't look as if my parents cared about my desire to become a psychiatrist and in the end, I intuitively felt that the reason I'd gotten pregnant was because a sweet little baby wanted to come into my life. Deep inside, I knew that my baby wanted to be born or I would not have become pregnant.

George and I got married a few weeks later in a small ceremony held at my parents' home. George's parents didn't attend. They were against us getting married because I was not Catholic, and we were not getting married in a Catholic church. They even questioned whether George was the father! I resented their judgment of the whole situation. However, about six months later in January of 1967 when our little girl was born, she was an exact match to George's side of the family. I may have given birth to her, but she so strongly resembled his family that they could no longer deny that George was the father.

According to George's parents, we were living in sin, not having been married in the Catholic Church. However, after seeing that our sweet little girl looked like their side of the family, George's parents decided to help us out by loaning us $6,000 to buy a tiny house. This was not just for a down payment. In 1967, $6,000 bought us the whole, VERY SMALL house! It was in Wyandotte, a city close to Grosse Ile, smack in the middle of a Polish neighborhood. I appreciated this loan as we didn't have a place to live, but I hated the location of the house that *they* had chosen for us. There were no young couples living close by but there were plenty of older people.

Every afternoon and evening, we would see several grandmas wearing babushkas sitting out on their front porches. Strict Catholic concepts were prevalent everywhere and I tried to feel accepted in this neighborhood. I purposefully kept to myself that I'd gotten pregnant out of wedlock and that we'd been married outside the Catholic Church!

As George went off to work every day in our only car, I quickly became very lonely, stuck in the house with a newborn. I played with our daughter and took care of her the best that I could. I read all the parenting books I could find and during her nap time I listened to soap operas which seemed to run all afternoon on the TV.

I started eating to comfort myself and as a result, never lost all the weight I'd gained during pregnancy. I was fifty pounds heavier than I'd been in high school when we met and because of this, George started criticizing me for being fat. My self-esteem got lower and lower. Of course, at that time in my life, I was unaware of how important it is to pay attention to your emotions. We both developed unhealthy habits to avoid the feelings we were having. I ate a lot and George started drinking more.

Addictions Begin

Monday through Friday, George began stopping after work at the bar with his work friends. He would come home an hour or two later and we fell into a pattern where I started becoming accustomed to his verbal abuse. In my mind, I felt I deserved to be yelled at because I was not the size, I'd been when we first met so I allowed myself to become his doormat. He would yell at me about my weight but still insist we have sex every night, which he felt he was entitled to, since he was the one going off to work every day. I resented having sex when I really didn't want to, but I didn't speak up, thinking that if I pleased him every night it would make him happy. I lied to myself and pretended that my desires didn't matter. My life had become pretty miserable.

Law of Attraction Principle

Thinking in a certain way over many years builds up a powerful momentum that can keep us stuck in a rut of misery. We can always change our experience in life, but it requires the awareness that it is our *thinking* that's attracting miserable situations to us. Without any knowledge of the Law of Attraction, it usually takes a defining moment or something very dramatic to happen before someone begins questioning their life and how or why things happen.

But there's one night I'll never forget. We'd invited a couple (long-time friends from high school) over to play cards. Having known each other for years, we were comfortable talking about anything and everything with each other. The guy made a comment that he wished his girlfriend would give him as much sex as I gave George. George blurted out, "Well, a lot of sex means nothing, especially when you're screwing a fat watermelon!"

I got up from the card table and ran to the bathroom. I cried silently for a while – but not for too long – as I didn't want anyone to know how much I was hurting from George's comment. When I came out, the subject quickly changed. The evening ended as it usually did, with our friends leaving and George insisting we have sex, despite my fat body!

Having sex was always the last thing I wanted, especially after a night of verbal abuse, as I felt so bad about my body. I felt constant turmoil within, confused as to why he would want to look at the same naked body he criticized so much. He often wanted me to put on sexy outfits like garter belts and stockings that he'd seen in the X-rated movies he loved. Being the people-pleaser that I was, I always put them on to make him happy, even though I never looked like the perfect bodies portrayed in those movies.

One evening, George decided to treat us to the pleasure of dining out. We chose a nice Italian restaurant because we both loved this kind of food. He ordered a delicious pasta dinner and I followed suit but suddenly, in front of the waitress, he immediately insisted that I change my order and select a fish dinner, so I would not get any fatter. With resentment, I did as he told me. Later, when we got home, he demanded sex, telling me to lie on my back so my stomach would not look as fat as when I kneeled. I felt worthless.

As a first-time mom – lonely, unhappy, and verbally abused – my self-esteem was at a low point. I felt so alone and unhappy that I even thought I somehow deserved this treatment.

Relief and Regret

Thoughts of fear or judgment are full of low-frequency energy. Because the Law of Attraction is always working, the results I attracted during those first three years of marriage were the low-frequency thoughts of depression, loneliness, and unworthiness.

Law of Attraction Principle

Simply stated, the Law of Attraction works like a mirror. It's always reflecting back to us how we are feeling. For instance, when we look into a mirror and we are crying, the reflection in the mirror will show us the exact emotion of the sadness and tears we're feeling in that moment. Babies love looking in mirrors to learn about themselves and thus we learn early on how the mirror reflects our exact feelings. The mirror is always consistent and so is the Law of Attraction.

Luckily, during those 3 years of misery, we had saved up enough money so George could finish getting his degree in automotive engineering. Things started getting better after we moved back to Kalamazoo. We lived in a small two-bedroom apartment (that was actually bigger than our house) in the married housing section on campus and my life began to feel better. It was wonderful to be around young married women who also had small children. My loneliness quickly disappeared. In talking with many mothers who had gained a lot of weight with their first pregnancies, I was introduced to Weight Watchers. I joined, found supportive friends, and learned how to make better food choices. Week by week, I began to lose weight. Eventually, I succeeded in losing the fifty pounds I'd gained from the pregnancy as well as the additional pounds I'd put on when eating to comfort myself in our first three years of marriage.

It felt so good to be back in the body I had in high school. I fit back into all the clothes in my closet, I had more energy, and my self-esteem and confidence about my appearance increased tremendously. This temporarily made George happy, but his sexual addiction continued to grow. He wanted more than just to see me wearing sexy lingerie. Now that he considered me attractive again, he decided he wanted to try "wife-swapping." He explained to me that it entailed finding another couple interested in trading partners for sexual pleasure. He told me that, since it would be an agreeable situation for all the people involved, it would not be considered cheating on one another.

None of this appealed to me at all. I had a hard-enough time enjoying sex with George, so I couldn't imagine having a good time in bed with a stranger. Thankfully I was thinner, and I wasn't as ashamed of my body as I had been, and since my people-pleasing habit was well-established by now, I went along with the wife swapping idea to make him happy.

The night finally arrived when George said he thought we should try to find a couple with whom to swap. We were invited to a party where many couples would be present and of course, drinking was a top priority at this party.

George began flirting with lots of girls, trying to narrow down which woman he might end up with who would have a partner willing to go along with this swapping idea. I was most comfortable talking with the other gals at the party and approaching other men was really out of my comfort zone. Eventually, I drank enough to give me the courage to approach an abandoned husband whose wife was busy with George.

I remember standing close to him in a hallway, talking with him, and eventually kissing him. Suddenly things backfired. Even though George had been busy all night hanging onto and kissing other women, he saw me kissing this man and became instantly jealous. He grabbed me, and we left the party. When we got home, he yelled at me and called me names. I remember screaming at him that he was crazy because it had been his idea in the first place. The argument ended as it always did with him insisting on sex. I hated the confusing life we were living! I woke up the next morning with the worst hangover I'd ever had and vowed never to drink myself into stupidity again. Luckily, wife-swapping didn't seem to appeal to George anymore and he never brought it up again.

I gave birth to our second child, our first son, while George was finishing his last two years of college. George had always wanted a boy, so I thought the birth of our son would finally brighten up his life, but nothing really changed. A second child certainly brought us more responsibilities and pressure. Money was tight, so George got a summer job as a door-to-door salesman and I began babysitting for other families to make ends meet. Having a baby boy didn't enhance our relationship or make George happier. It seemed like there was nothing I could do that would have ever please him. He drank more to ignore his unhappiness but luckily, not enough to interfere with his studies.

George finally graduated from college with a degree in automotive engineering and had the pleasure of being hired back at the auto company in Detroit where he had started working right out of high school. His new position required us to move to the state of Oklahoma.

Never happy within himself, and with his wife-swapping idea backfiring on him due to his own jealousy, George eventually began to search for sex outside of our marriage. This began when we lived for two years in Oklahoma City when he traveled a lot. For two-week stretches at a time he worked in another city and being away from home made it easy and convenient for him to have an extramarital affair. I was totally unaware of this affair until eventually, he decided to be up-front and tell me. At that point, he'd conveniently been given a new position at work and we were being transferred to a very small town in Wisconsin. I was very hurt but moving away from that woman to a whole new state made it easier for me to believe that he would stop cheating on me. It also made it easier for me to ignore the truth, that our marriage needed help.

I was really fooling myself expecting our marriage to get better without changing any of our old habits. Moving to a new location didn't change my low self-esteem nor the feeling of unworthiness that I'd had for so many years and George continued to drink.

Focus on the Good Things in Life

There was one thing that I did enjoy about our marriage – the love that my children and I shared. I loved being a mom. My kids were so adorable and irresistible to me. I read every book that I could find on how to be a good mother. The feeling of unconditional love that my children and I shared brought me so much happiness. I found myself focusing on that aspect of my life because it felt good. It helped me to ignore the painful truth about how unhappy I was being married to George.

I'd learned that there were also many other things that I could do to keep me happy while raising our kids. I learned to bowl and joined a ladies' bowling league. I learned to play tennis and enjoyed this sport while the kids were in school. I read self-help and parenting books and I joined book discussion groups. I belonged to mothers' groups where we traded babysitting, so each mom could have some free time to herself. Besides these fun things, I also cooked, cleaned, mowed the lawn, took the garbage out, and did all the grocery shopping. All this activity kept me busy, fairly happy, and able to tolerate my life. This was the main reason that I could pretend that our marriage was doing okay, despite the truth that our relationship lacked any intimacy, productive communication, or respect for one another.

In Oklahoma I was using an IUD to prevent another pregnancy but just before we moved to Wisconsin, I got pregnant anyway. A few days before the moving truck came to haul all our belongings away, I started experiencing cramps. After several hours of cramping and bleeding, the fetus, along with the IUD, came out. I had miscarried. After the doctor had checked me, he told me to be sure and follow up with a physician once we arrived at our new home. I had no time to feel sad or even recover before we were in the car and driving to Wisconsin.

George insisted on sex almost every night, so after the move, with no birth control protection, and before I even had a chance to find a gynecologist, I got pregnant. Nine months later, I gave birth to our third child, a boy. When our baby was just one week old, George got another promotion and we were suddenly transferred to Boston, Massachusetts. Once again, we packed our things and drove across the country to the East Coast.

The two years that we lived in the Boston area went by quickly and looking back, those two years were the most enjoyable of our twenty-year marriage. George didn't travel, he cut down on his drinking, and we made a lot of friends. Many of our friends were couples. We played in bridge groups and were involved in various other social activities. It was a small, short-lived taste of what an enjoyable marriage could be like, and I ended up seven months pregnant with our fourth child just before we got news of our last transfer. I'd always wanted four children, so I was happy to be pregnant and I was also thankful that this transfer was back to our home state of Michigan.

PART THREE:

The Awakening

A New Chapter Begins

We found a nice home with a big yard and four bedrooms in a newly-developed subdivision in the small town of Novi, (pronounced Nov-eye) a suburb of Detroit. It was perfect for our growing family and I was happy to give birth to our last beautiful baby boy two months after we moved back. Knowing how easily I got pregnant, how unstable my life was, and that the IUD didn't effectively prevent pregnancy, I quickly had my tubes tied right after the delivery.

I loved our new house and being the mom of our four children! At this point, our daughter was eleven and our three sons were eight, two, and newborn. I got busy, as usual, by joining a Newcomers' club, where I found ways to enjoy my days with moms' support groups, book-discussion groups, and anything else that made me happy.

The good years we experienced in Boston quickly began to fade as George got busy working long hours. He eventually resumed his old habit of stopping for a drink with his buddies after work. On the weekends, he would spend many hours away from home, golfing on Saturdays and then coming home to crash on the couch for the rest of the evening. He always spent Sundays watching sports and napping on the couch. I wasn't happy with his self-absorbed weekends but if I complained, nothing changed anyway, so I kept quiet about my feelings. I continued to do everything myself, allowing him to sleep on the couch and skip participating in family chores or excursions. Thus, I enabled our miserable mess of a marriage to continue with no improvement.

About three years after we had moved back to Michigan, I got a call from Lyn, a good friend of mine from the Boston area. She was really excited about a part-time job she'd found selling UndercoverWear lingerie at home parties, making great money and having fun at the same time. She said it was perfect for her because she could stay at home with her two girls during the day and go out for three hours in the evening, making an average of $100 a night. In addition, she had earned an all-expenses-paid trip to Aruba from UndercoverWear. I was happy for her and congratulated her on her new-found career.

Lyn knew that since we had moved back to Michigan, I'd been unhappy in my marriage and felt as if I was raising the four children by myself. She also knew that George was either gone all the time or sleeping on the couch. Because I liked to laugh and have fun, just like the women at her UndercoverWear parties did, she thought I should try doing what she was doing as well.

Although it's very true that I do love to laugh and have fun with the girls, my initial thoughts about this idea were full of doubt and worry as I knew nothing about lingerie OR sales. In fact, I couldn't see how I would ever get bookings because when I had attended any home parties, I couldn't stand the pushy salespeople. With four kids running around and a drunken husband showing up at any time during the evening, I would never book a show myself because I didn't want women coming into my home. In addition, asking George for money to do something just for me was unheard of at that point in our marriage. Asking for $300 to buy a starter kit, let alone asking him to come home to babysit for our four children in the evening, was a scary thought.

Lyn assured me that if I did not like it, I could simply quit. As the good supportive friend that she was, she said she'd buy my kit back if I chose to quit, which was not UndercoverWear policy at all.

Well, I decided I had nothing to lose, so I got my courage up and asked George for the money. Not understanding the power of my thoughts back in those days, I got exactly what I expected from him: a lot of criticism and complaining. I can easily remember how it unfolded. He said, "You want to do what? Sell lingerie at home parties? What does that mean?"

And I said, "Well, it's sort of like Tupperware but a lot more fun! My friend Lyn's been doing this for about a year and as a result, she's earned an all-expenses-paid trip to Aruba for herself and her husband."

He immediately jumped into criticism: "Why should I give you the money? You'll never be successful! You know nothing about lingerie, you know nothing about sales and you're way too fat to be successful!" It was true that over the years of comforting myself by eating, combined with a few more pregnancies, I'd gained back the weight I'd lost while George was getting his degree. George didn't like the weight gain, so I wasn't surprised at what he said. I became quiet as I knew by this time that arguing with an alcoholic is hopeless and that he would just become more verbally abusive.

Law of Attraction Principle

We take ourselves wherever we go. Since like attracts like, unless we change our habits of thought, we will keep attracting the same experiences along the way.

Instead of my normal self-doubt and negative self-talk, in this moment of quiet, I thought silently to myself, "If you give me the money, I will be successful." It is true that I didn't know *how* I'd become successful and I didn't know when, but I had a strong desire and an unusual feeling of confidence that it would work out, given the chance.

After several minutes of silence, he finally said, "Fine, I'll give you the money, but you'll never be successful!" I took it, and thus my journey into the unknown had begun. No one else was selling UndercoverWear in Michigan so I couldn't go to a party or see how to do it. We didn't have a catalog, training material, or even a website like companies have today, so the way I began to learn was by calling my friend Lyn and asking for help.

Fear

I quickly realized that I had fears I'd never even thought about. I was no longer just a mom – I was an UndercoverWear agent! Yes, it's a fun and catchy title that UndercoverWear had decided we'd call ourselves instead of "party plan demonstrators". The first fear I had to overcome was getting comfortable talking in front of a group of people. Throughout our life together, George had been the big social butterfly, the talker, and storyteller at parties. I'd always been happy to be quiet, listen, and laugh, so this role reversal was difficult.

I began to have headaches through the first few shows, which was the result of stress, worry and fear. I was not aware of the Law of Attraction at that time, but I ended up intuitively attracting a solution.

During the party, UndercoverWear agents gave the women attending a fun game to play called the Sensuality Test. UndercoverWear supplied us with a list of sensual questions to ask the ladies who got points for their answers. After ten questions, both the highest and the lowest scorers were given a prize, so no one felt like a loser. The questions went something like, "Have you ever greeted your favorite male at the door wearing sexy lingerie? If you have, you get twenty points. If not, give yourself a zero."

After several shows, I realized that when I asked the questions that made *me* laugh the most, I didn't notice my headache. By about the fifth show, I'd overcome the headaches and the fear of speaking in front of a group because I'd raised the frequency of my energy field by selecting only questions that made me laugh.

When I chose to allow myself to have fun at the party by picking the questions I liked, rather than living in fear of not doing a good job, things changed. In fact, this is exactly how the Law of Attraction works. New thoughts brought me new results. It's hard – in fact, it's impossible – to hold on to a headache when you're laughing and having fun! In summary, I stopped focusing on what I didn't want and started focusing on what I did want.

Law of Attraction Principle

By shifting our focus, we can prove to ourselves that we can change our experiences in life by changing our thoughts.

The next fear I had to overcome was finding the courage to ask people to book a party. I was afraid of rejection because I remembered never wanting to book a show at any home party I'd attended. I was assuming that other women probably felt as I did so I never asked anyone at the parties if they wanted to book a show. The only way I was getting any bookings was when I'd personally ask my close friends or family if they would mind doing me a favor and having a show for me.

The Power of Thought

In 1981, about three months into my UndercoverWear career, I got a call from a woman who wrote articles for the women's section in *The Detroit News.* This was the most popular newspaper that everyone around the Metro Detroit area read. She wanted to see an UndercoverWear show and write an article about this new and innovative home party plan experience. I was nervous about the whole idea and had no idea what to expect from a journalist.

Law of Attraction Principle

Our inner being, or gut instinct, is always guiding us. The key is allowing ourselves to feel our true emotion before making any decisions. If we wait until it feels right to make a decision, we will attract the good-feeling results we want.

Since I was just getting over the headaches and my fear of speaking, I postponed allowing her to attend a party for about a month. Finally, it felt right, and I called her and invited her to the next show.

While she was at the party, she acted very serious. She took lots of notes and she never smiled, even during the fun sensuality test! When it was over, she thanked me for letting her be there and said she wasn't sure when she was going to publish the article but that it would be "sometime in the future." I was relieved and hoped she'd never print it. I thought her serious demeanor meant that she hadn't had a good time and that it wouldn't be a very favorable article.

A few months later, much to my surprise, she called me and told me she had decided that the perfect time to print the article would be Mother's Day, in *The Detroit Sunday News*. I did not foresee the amazing experience that was to come.

Law of Attraction Principle

Once we make a decision, line up with it, and don't worry about the outcome. If we feel good when we make the decision, the Universe will bring us what we want in any number of delightful ways. Letting go of the outcome, helps us begin to prove to ourselves that the Universe will support us when we feel good.

Even though I had been fearful of the consequences, I decided to let go of the worry and allow her to attend the party and eventually publish the article. By doing so, I learned that letting go of fear opens the door for us to receive all the rendezvous that the Universe has lined up for us.

My fear of the article having a negative impact was unfounded. It was very well written and was complete with pictures. It covered the front page, as well as page two, of the women's section in the paper's Mother's Day special. Before the article was published, I had never received a single booking as the result of a party. After it came out, my phone started ringing off the wall (and yes, it really was hooked to the wall. There were no handy cell phones in those days!) Over the course of the next few weeks, I had so many phone calls that I lost count.

The amazing thing that I learned about myself and the power of my thoughts at that time was that all the women calling to book a party were giving me the gift of a new perspective that was helping me to eliminate my fear of rejection when asking for bookings. All these wonderful strangers were saying: "I saw the article in *The Detroit News* about your UndercoverWear parties and I was wondering if you would *do me a favor* and come to my house to have a party for me and my friends!" This experience was a major turning point in my career; I had an "Aha" moment when I realized that *I* was doing *them* a favor as opposed to thinking that they were doing one for me.

Law of Attraction Principle

Perspective is everything. When we think about something and purposefully choose thoughts that cause us to feel better about the situation, we change our results!

I finally realized that I was giving everyone a wonderful evening by doing a show for them, not just taking up their time. The newspaper article, along with the change in my thinking, set me free to attract many good things into my life and within three years, I was making as much money as my husband!

I was having so much fun at the parties and enjoyed being with the girls at each show that I looked at the shows as my own fun girls' night out. I loved helping women to laugh and have a fun evening, and I loved giving them the opportunity to shop in the comfort of a living room. They appreciated my being there, so they could try on lingerie and intimate apparel in the privacy of a home rather than in a cold dressing room in a store. They also got to treat themselves to a night without worries. For a few hours, we all forgot any stress in our lives. We focused on ourselves and the power of bonding, laughing, and feeling good. Most of the time, the bookings came easily for the rest of my twenty-five-year career with UndercoverWear and so did the recruits. Women would come up to me and say, "Wow, you're having so much fun and making money too; I think I'd like to do this!" or, "I'd like to have a show and share this with my friends!"

Law of Attraction Principle

When we love what we do, and we are passionate about it, the Universe will bring us the results we want.

This shift in my thought process allowed me to attract more bookings and recruits. This led to more money and many bonuses including twenty-five, all-expenses-paid trips to destinations all around the world just by doing what I loved.

Loving and Hating!

Within three years, I'd built a structure which included fifteen managers and a hundred and fifty UndercoverWear agents. I loved this successful feeling!

I often held meetings and training programs in my home. One of those meetings fell on my birthday. Much to my dismay, for the first time in our marriage, George had not come home the night before the meeting. Yes, he had cheated on me before, but he had never blatantly stayed out all night long. He came into the house during the morning meeting, making his appearance look normal to everyone, as if he'd gone out early in the morning to get me a present. He handed me a rose and wished me a happy birthday. I was stunned. I knew I had to continue with my meeting, so I conveniently pushed my feelings aside. I pretended that this was a nice gesture on his part, even though I assumed he was back to cheating on me, since he'd been out all night.

Later that night, George and I went bowling. When the evening was over, and we got home, I finally had the courage to confront him on his whereabouts the previous night. He admitted that he'd been with a woman and that he had done it because she was thinner than me. I ran to the bathroom and cried. Eventually, I came out screaming at him about how much I hated our sick marriage!

Since I was making as much money as George, I had the courage to tell him that we needed to either work on our marriage or get a divorce. We tried counseling for many months, both for our own sake as well as the sake of our children. The psychiatrist we saw helped us considerably but unfortunately, George was not ready to admit that he had a drinking problem. He did not feel responsible for any of the things that had gone wrong with our marriage and after about a year of trying, I saw there was no hope of him changing. When the psychiatrist asked me, "What kind of role models do you want your children to see in a husband and wife?" I knew that we needed to divorce.

Toward the end of our marriage, things became difficult because George said he didn't want the divorce but neither did he want to change his behavior. He would often come home late from work or from a bar, delaying me from leaving for an UndercoverWear party. Running late, I would feel worried and stressed as I drove across town in the rush-hour traffic. When I came home at around ten in the evening, I'd find him asleep on the couch and all the kids asleep on the floor, still in their clothes. As a mom, I felt guilty leaving the kids with a father who appeared not to care.

This provided me with an opportunity to learn something that has helped me ever since. I had seen enough of my own team of agents struggling with the fact that no one enjoys being around a grumpy, worried, or complaining salesperson at any home party. When I left the house for a party, I knew I needed, and wanted, to change my mood before I arrived. As soon as I pulled out of my driveway, I would put on an inspirational or motivational recording from one of the popular speakers and authors of the time, such as Tony Robbins, Zig Ziglar, Napoleon Hill, or Earl Nightingale.

When I listened to others' inspiring words, I quickly noticed how my mood would begin to change. The longer I listened, the better I felt. My stress and worry went away and by the time I arrived at a party, I was a different person. I also realized that I could really perk up my energy by putting on some of my favorite upbeat music for ten to fifteen minutes. You know, the kind of music that makes you want to chair-dance (bouncing in your seat to the beat of the music) while you're driving! These things helped me to temporarily set aside my mess of a family situation I had going on in my life. When I arrived, I would be a happy woman, glad to be able to enjoy a fun girls' night out and make money, too!

So, what had I learned? I'd learned that my thoughts (including those from inspirational speakers) produced my emotions. If you want to change the results you're getting in life, begin by paying attention to your emotions.

Law of Attraction Principle

Our emotions are always indicating the results we will be attracting. When we're feeling down and realize we don't want to feel this way, we can choose to listen to someone else's uplifting words or our favorite upbeat music. This helps raise our own energy to a higher frequency, which allows us to begin to feel better. When we feel better, we attract better feeling results.

Happiness for me at that time was having more bookings and more recruits. Learning how to feel good while running my business, despite the circumstances of my marriage, was powerful. In the 1980s and 1990s, "a positive mental attitude" was a popular phrase promoted by authors and speakers. I certainly understood the value of thinking positively in my life. However, it wasn't until 2007, when I learned about the Law of Attraction, that I began to understand that negative thoughts are just as attractive and powerful as positive ones.

Freedom

After almost twenty years of marriage, George and I finally got divorced. I became the single parent of our four children for about ten years which, along with running my UndercoverWear business, kept me very busy. I continued to read books on personal growth, sales, and parenting. I felt confident as a mom, as a salesperson, and as an UndercoverWear divisional leader, but I must admit that there was one area in my life where I didn't feel confident: the area of relationships between men and women. My parents had made relationships look so easy, but my own experience left me doubting that I could ever have what my parents had. Since I didn't know the value of paying attention to my emotions, I didn't know that the doubt I kept buried inside of me was keeping me from attracting a good relationship. Since I felt good about myself in the areas of childrearing and business, I got results that felt the same way.

However, I had no good feeling thoughts on me ever having a good relationship with a man which is why I continued to attract bad ones for the next decade. I hadn't yet learned the importance of improving my own self esteem before moving into a new relationship. I didn't understand that *like attracts like* and so I continued to ignore or discount my thoughts of low self-worth that I'd acquired over 20 years of verbal abuse and my own negative self-talk.

Law of Attraction Principle

Our emotions are our own personal guidance system, just like the GPS in a car that guides us to our destination. When we feel good, we're headed in the right direction toward our desires, because the high-frequency energy we're emitting will attract high-frequency, good-feeling results. When we feel bad, our emotions are warning us that we are headed in the wrong direction. Buried or unconscious emotions are still present and powerful within us so when we ignore our bad feeling emotions, we inadvertently will attract bad feeling experiences.

A year after my divorce was finalized, a girlfriend reminded me that my whole life revolved around being with women and raising my kids. She thought we should go to a bar once in a while so that I would have the chance to meet a man. I honestly didn't care about finding a man. I was happy doing what I loved and being a single parent. But my people-pleasing habits were still strong at that point in my life, so I went along with her concern about my future loneliness and began going out to a bar with her every now and then.

True Colors

The poet and award-winning author Maya Angelou once said to Oprah Winfrey, "When someone shows you who they really are, believe them!" I heard Oprah share this with her audience on a program honoring Maya after her death. Looking back on my life, I wish I'd heard those words of wisdom in 1986, but of course I know that even if I had, I wouldn't have been ready to receive Maya Angelou's sound advice.

I did eventually meet a guy named Jason in a bar. He was funny and entertaining, and because I enjoyed talking and laughing with others, I decided to ignore the fact that he drank twice as much as me every evening that we were together. He told me that his parents had always picked on him and yelled at him. While he was growing up, his dad beat him with a belt for no reason at all, but not his two brothers. He was labeled the black sheep of the family. I'm sure his own self-worth was about as low as mine. In hindsight, I realize how the Law of Attraction brought us together. Remember, energy always attracts like energy, and the Law of Attraction is always working, whether we're aware of it or not. As a result, here were two people who both had low self-esteem being drawn together in life. I didn't understand that I was leading myself into the same kind of relationship that I had attracted the first time around as a teen. Shakespeare was right when he wrote, "All the world's a stage." I was staging my own repeat performance of being attracted to an alcoholic.

I pretended it didn't matter, so I chose to overlook Jason's excessive drinking. I dated him for ten years which gave me plenty of time to get to know him. Early on in our relationship, signs that he was irresponsible, and a liar showed up. I was familiar with lies and deceit from my first marriage experience. I hadn't yet realized how my thoughts about men would attract the same kind of partner I drew to myself before, or that I could attract a different type of man by changing my thoughts. No wonder I attracted Jason!

The first time we had sex, we discussed the fact that I couldn't get pregnant as I'd had my tubes tied. We didn't use any protection. Three days after our first sexual experience, I went to the doctor to see what was causing me so much pain. When I found out that I'd contracted an STD, I was dumbfounded! Discussions about sexually transmitted diseases were not prevalent in those days and it was certainly the last thing I thought I needed to consider. I hadn't even considered bringing the subject up with Jason.

When I told him of my diagnosis, he immediately claimed that I couldn't have gotten it from him and accused me of having sex with someone else. Of course, I knew that this was ridiculous and felt confused as to what to do. He adamantly refused to admit he'd given me an STD. I suddenly felt trapped in a big mess. I began to think that no other man would ever want to be with me again, because I had been told that this condition never goes away and can easily be passed on to others. Once again, my self-esteem plummeted. I didn't talk to Jason for a few weeks, but he kept calling. Ignoring my gut feeling that I should stay away from him, I decided to see him again because of my belief that I was a loser and no one else would want me.

Another quote I love from Maya Angelou is: "When you know better, you do better." At that time in my life, I didn't know any other way to handle relationships, so I unconsciously settled for less. I had settled for less in my first marriage and since I didn't know any better, I continued this pattern into the second marriage.

A few weeks after the STD diagnosis, I started seeing Jason again. One evening when we were together at his house, he answered a phone call. His face turned pale and his voice cracked. When I asked him what was wrong, he said that I must promise never to tell anyone. I agreed, and he proceeded to tell me that the woman who called had just given birth to his child, a little girl. He went on to tell me that this woman had asked him to get her pregnant, as she was getting older and wanted a child but wanted to remain single. He said they had made an agreement that she would not hold him responsible for helping to raise the baby in any way. Whether it was the truth or a lie I didn't know at that time. But the one thing I did know for sure was that, throughout our eighteen years together, he insisted that I never tell the truth to his family or to anyone that he had any children.

When his daughter reached her teens, the courts eventually caught up with him and he was required to pay child support, including arrearages. He told no one except me about this and continued with his usual lie when someone brought up the subject of children. If asked, the answer was always a definite, "No". It was clear to me at that point that habitual lying was part of his character but because I was used to settling for less, I decided to lower my values and carry on with this lie for years. I hated lying about it because I loved my children so much and never understood how anyone could choose to ignore their child and lie about it so easily.

Over the years, Jason's sense of humor began to irritate me. He often made fun of fat people and deep inside, I continued to struggle with my own self-image. I learned very well how to pretend that these jokes, and everything else that was bothering me, didn't really matter, and I continued to turn to food to comfort myself. My weight went up and down and I became one of those many people who try every fad diet around. Of course, they always worked temporarily, but eventually I would return to my usual eating habits and regain the weight.

Many years into our relationship, Jason asked me if I would be interested in working part-time for his parents' small, mom-and-pop business. He'd become the salesperson and his mom and dad stayed in the office and ran the business. They were getting old and his mom didn't want to learn how to do the bookkeeping on a computer. Everything was handwritten in logbooks and he hoped I would come in and help her with all the paperwork. Since my kids were getting older, I had free time during the day to help, so I began working there part-time. Within about three years, I was very familiar with all the products they sold and knew how to handle all the bookkeeping for the business. During that time, because I was distracted by Jason and working in his family business, I paid little attention to my UndercoverWear business, which gradually got smaller. Eventually, his mother needed a hip replacement and left work. As a result, I began to work forty hours a week for his family. I continued my career with UndercoverWear, but I wasn't focusing on it. Little by little, it became less profitable.

After I'd worked with Jason for five years, I'd gotten to know his parents well and had become friends with them. They were delighted that I'd learned so much about their products and bookkeeping since I'd started working there. I had proven my ability to be reliable and accountable which was totally opposite to the experience they'd had with Jason and his progression into alcoholism. Of course, no one in their family ever talked about it his addiction and I was subconsciously ignoring all the signs. When we announced that we were getting married they were thrilled. Within a year after getting married, they decided to retire and give Jason their company.

I was very happy about this because I'd spent a big portion of my time and energy helping grow their business. As Jason's wife, I was officially part owner, and this gave me a comfortable feeling of security. My UndercoverWear business continued to get smaller as I decided to focus on our company in which I was now so deeply involved.

A few months after his parents retired, Jason began drinking more and more. As soon as they were out of the picture, he no longer had to come back to the office to report to his father about the clients he'd called on or taken out to lunch. Going out to lunch became the starting point of his daily drinking and he began coming back to the office smelling of booze. This got progressively worse and I finally began to admit to myself that I'd made a big mistake with this second marriage. I decided to ignore my own happiness, as I'd done so many times before, and began to think that all I needed to do was work hard to build this business and keep my UndercoverWear as a side job. I figured that within four to five years of hard work, I could grow the business, and then we could sell it and retire at a young age. I thought that when we retired, I would finally have a chance to be happy. Sadly, I was again postponing my happiness until sometime in the future. I had become the ultimate master of living in denial.

Law of Attraction Principle

When our day-to-day living conditions are unhappy, we cannot attract a happy ending.

What I didn't know back then is that working hard and pushing through pain prevents you from attracting good-feeling results because pain and happiness do not have the same vibration. Putting off my happiness for the future was keeping me stuck in a bad situation and so the happy future could never come. When we're living in denial and ignoring the pain through drinking, overeating, overworking, etc., what we attract is more pain. Since I didn't know about the Law of Attractison, I didn't know that *you cannot attract a happy ending to an unhappy journey.*

PART FOUR:

The Shift

The Future Never Comes

The fateful day arrived: the phone rang, and I found out that Jason had been living a double life. I immediately felt a gigantic knot in my stomach. I felt like throwing up. But like I'd done my entire life, I swallowed the excruciating pain. When I finally got home, I fell to the floor and cried my heart out while my sweet dog Roxie licked my tears. After I was exhausted from crying, I felt a little relief. I took a deep breath and felt a calm come over me. I became aware that there was something more about me and my life that I didn't understand. I'd been married twice. These marriages were to two different men and had spanned two different times in my life. The one thing I knew for sure was that I was the one common ingredient in both long and unhappy marriages. I asked myself, "What about me do I need to change and what do I need to learn about life so I never have to experience another painful relationship?"

Law of Attraction Principle

When we are faced with a challenge and do not know what to do next, the Law of Attraction will not allow us to find the answer immediately. When we state the question, we are focusing on the problem, which has a lower vibration than the answer. The key to attracting the solution is to stop looking at the problem and to simply find ways to make ourselves feel better. The solution will always be found in a higher vibrational state or thought pattern where all good feelings exist.

I certainly didn't receive an answer right away. I didn't understand the value of becoming quiet and listening to my inner being or gut instinct at that time in my life. Instead, I began focusing on the main problem I was facing; I knew right away that I wanted to find out everything I could about Jason's deceitful ways.

After several weeks of detective work, I discovered that Jason had purchased a house for his girlfriend a year earlier. What surprised me even more was that he'd bought this house for her the same year that we'd purchased a timeshare in Hawaii. We had hoped to take yearly vacations in the future. I guess he'd assumed I would never find out about his double life if we kept planning vacations and pretending all was well. Yes, I knew our relationship wasn't satisfying for either of us. We never talked about anything but the business we ran together. When we finally talked about enjoying this timeshare and yearly vacations as we got older, I never suspected that he had any plans other than to share his future with me. I knew I wasn't happy with him because of his alcoholism but I'd thought that in a few short years we could sell the business and retire and then I could start having fun.

Looking back on it now, I see that I was postponing my enjoyment of a fun life. What I learned from that is how important it is to live in the NOW! Allow yourself to feel good in the present and do not wait for happiness to come sometime in the future.

When I confronted Jason about the house and his girlfriend, amazingly he said he didn't want a divorce. He expected me to believe that he'd bought the house so that this homeless young woman and her two children would have a place to live. He said he felt his purchase was an investment in rental property and didn't think I needed to know the details. He told me that he believed that what I didn't know wouldn't hurt me. At first, I thought I would feel better if he would admit the truth and tell me he loved me and that he was sorry and that he'd made a mistake. I thought these words would somehow help me overlook the pain I was feeling and forgive him. This is a sad example of how insecure and addicted to living in pain I was.

He never did say he was sorry but in hindsight it was meant to unfold in this way because I was forced to accept the truth that my life was at a turning point. Putting my head in the sand was not going to work anymore!

I had allowed Jason to manipulate me for years. I think he was hoping to have his cake and eat it too. He wanted us to stay married and have me run the business. He wanted me to continue to overlook his deceit as I'd been doing for years and pretend nothing had happened. He used temper tantrums to try to pressure me into forgiving him. He did a great job of getting a tear in his eye and attempting to excuse his actions as the result of having Post-Traumatic Stress Disorder from serving in Vietnam. In the 18 years I'd known him, he'd never once mentioned having PTSD so at this point, I decided that habitual liars and manipulators will say anything and everything to get you to eventually break down and say yes.

Several months dragged on in what looked like a hopeless situation. Instead of listening to my heart, I debated in my mind what to do. Eventually, I found out through more research that she had never paid him any rent during the nine months she'd lived in the house.

Jason owned two homes: the one he'd lived in before I met him and the one he'd bought for the girlfriend. The marital home that we lived in was mine before we met and was in my name only. When I found out about his double life, I asked him to move into one of his other houses. Used to getting his way, he said he would not do it because he "didn't have the heart to kick out the renters", as they would have nowhere to go. Besides, he knew he could easily continue living with me. At that point, he probably knew that the court system in Michigan only allows a spouse to kick the abusive partner out of the marital home when the abuse is physical. Since what I was going through was "only" mental or emotional abuse, I was unable to force him to move into one of his other houses, which really made life difficult from that point on.

Jason continued to abuse me verbally at work and at home in his effort to convince me to stay married to him. He even went to the extreme of having our home phone, a landline, wiretapped so he could listen in on any conversations I was having. By listening in on my discussions with my sisters he always knew how weak, vulnerable and insecure I was. Months later, when I hired an attorney, he listened in on all my phone discussions with her, which of course helped him to plan his own defense and more ways to manipulate me.

At that point in my life, my feelings about relationships were very negative. Of course, I felt like the unlucky victim of verbal abuse and deception, because I certainly would never have asked for such relationships.

I thought I was a victim because I had not learned that the abuser and the victim have the same energy field due to their low self-esteem and their self-criticism. Jason led a double life and lashed out at me due to his bad feelings about himself, and I ignored the bad feelings about myself and accepted the abuse. Oftentimes, like me, victims can feel so bad about themselves that they subconsciously feel they deserve it. They may also fear confrontation and the resulting additional abuse it can bring. This is how, unknowingly, victims and abusers remain stuck in a rut of misery.

Law of Attraction Principle

The energy we are emitting (based on the emotion we are feeling) attracts back identical energy to us in the form of thoughts and experiences. In this way, the Law of Attraction is similar to a boomerang. When we throw a boomerang off the rooftop of a building, it always comes back to where we are standing on the rooftop. Similarly, when we think high-frequency, or positive-feeling thoughts, we will always attract positive-feeling thoughts and experiences. Because both victims and abusers regularly send out low-frequency, or negative-feeling thoughts, they tend to attract negative-feeling experiences, and as such, often rendezvous with each other.

It's important to remember that no one actually chooses to become a victim. It happens by default because the law of attraction is always working whether we know about it or not. Like attracts like and there are no exceptions to this universal law. The negative energy of an abuser is identical to the negative energy of the victim every time. It is a hard concept to swallow because it's not easy to become accountable for our own misery. Accountability, without self-judgment, is the very beginning of learning how to attract a better life.

Aha Moment!

When I found out that the woman living in the house he secretly owned had never paid any rent, it confirmed to me that she was more than a renter. I knew I had to decide to move forward. I had so many fears at that time. I was truly worried about how I was ever going to get through this and keep my wits about me. Then a memory popped into my mind. It was about the time, many months back, when I had fallen to my knees crying and sobbing and thought, "What do I need to learn about life, and myself, so that I never repeat another painful relationship?"

After remembering this emotional moment and the question I'd asked myself, I sat quietly and realized I was ready to accept the mess my life was in. With this awareness, two more thoughts came to me that felt like the next logical step for me to take. First, I knew that I had to call my friend and mentor, Tiffany James, the CEO of UndercoverWear who had helped me so much over the last 25 years. Second, I knew that I needed to find an attorney.

Law of Attraction Principle

To attract something better, we must first make peace with the current situation that we do not like.

When you're stuck in a rut of unhappiness, one of the best ways to help yourself move forward and use the Law of Attraction for leverage is to accept and make peace with the truth of your situation. The first step in finding peace is to acknowledge the true emotion you are feeling and allow yourself to feel it deeply and feel it for as long as it takes until you notice your pain subsiding. When you respect and honor your true emotions, you're no longer living in denial or lying to yourself. This may mean (in the privacy of your own home with no one else around) crying and screaming and yelling until you're exhausted. You may even want to punch a pillow or beat a punching bag to release the pent-up energy of depression and/ or anger. You've been carrying this heavy burden for so long that you'll recognize when you're at peace with your situation because you will begin to feel some relief. At this point, you may find yourself instinctively taking a deep breath of fresh air. This deep breath instantly connects you with the Source energy of the universe.

When you're truly at peace, the rut you were stuck in no longer exists. The Law of Attraction simultaneously allows you to rendezvous with higher frequency energy. This is when you will begin to hear your inner being or inner guidance. When your inner being speaks to you, it will be calm and gentle and will feel like the next logical step to take at this point in your life.

I called Tiffany. I told her that, even though I had earned an all-expenses-paid trip for two to Puerto Vallarta, Mexico, I wasn't going to be able to take it: I was starting divorce proceedings against my husband and I was too upset and confused to see myself taking a vacation at this turning point in my life. When she heard what had happened, she was pleased. She shared with me that no one in UndercoverWear could ever understand how or why I stayed with a man who was so controlling and verbally abusive to me. She said, "I still want you to come on the trip. You've earned it and you deserve it. But most importantly, I want to support you, so I'm going to help you find a good attorney." Tiffany had given me many gifts throughout my years with UndercoverWear and I had appreciated every one of them. However, the attorney she found for me was the greatest gift she could ever have given me.

Shannon was a woman who had been in UndercoverWear many years previously. I had seen her as my competitor as she'd developed a large structure that was more productive than mine. In the early days of my career, I had also felt inferior to her. My first husband George had always made snide comments to me that the only reason she was more successful than me was because she was thin and I was fat.

She left UndercoverWear because she had contracted the Epstein-Barr virus, also known as Chronic Fatigue Syndrome, and I'd lost touch with her. She had become an attorney and had been successfully helping people get divorces for more than fifteen years.

Her office was forty-five minutes from my house, much farther than I wanted to drive, but I trusted Tiffany's promise that if I didn't feel comfortable with her or didn't like the long drive, Shannon would be happy to refer me to another divorce attorney in my area.

I was happy to discover that I felt very comfortable with Shannon. We certainly weren't competitors anymore, and I felt her confidence and her sincere desire to help me. She told me she would be happy to take my case on as long as I promised to do everything she recommended. This made good sense to me as I knew I really didn't know where to begin, so I agreed.

I was totally surprised that the first thing she wanted me to do was to learn how to meditate. She said she wanted me to learn a specific kind of meditation that Deepak Chopra taught called Primordial Sound Meditation. She had been meditating for years and found it very helpful for relieving stress. I told her that I'd read about meditation and logically understood the value in it, but I could never get my mind to become quiet. She said she didn't want me to try to do it on my own, that a class setting would be better for me, and that she was going to find a teacher who taught this type of meditation.

I hesitated about that idea. At that point in my life, I was spending many hours on the road. My drive to work every day took twenty minutes each way. To save money for the divorce, I had started holding more UndercoverWear parties in the evenings which always included a thirty to forty-five-minute drive each way. Shannon's office was another long forty-five minutes to an hour away. When she said she wanted to find a meditation teacher for me, I said, "Fine, but I really don't want to drive to Clarkston (where her office was located) to learn how to meditate." My life was in a turmoil and just the thought of driving way across town to learn how to meditate sounded like it would add even more stress to my life.

Law of Attraction Principle

Pre-pave our experiences daily by setting our intentions about how we would like the results to feel before we embark on something. Getting into the feeling place first, sets up the vibrational atmosphere that allows us to rendezvous with the good feeling results we are looking for.

To use the Law of Attraction effectively, you need to clearly set your intentions, let them go out to the Universe and know in your heart that the

Universe will line up the desired experience to meet your expectation. This is exactly what my attorney did.

Even though I was complaining about driving a long way, Shannon said it was no problem. She took a deep breath and set her intention. She opened the phone book and within a short amount of time, found a woman within a mile of me who taught exactly what she wanted me to learn. I was somewhat reluctant since I really didn't think I could get my mind to become quiet but, since the class was only a mile from my house, I agreed to go.

Empowerment Begins

When I called to register, I was lucky to find that there was just one space left and that I could have it. Yes, the Universe had already lined this up for me! The class would start in a month. At that time, spirituality was the one area in my life that I knew I hadn't focused on much. Since Shannon seemed so confident about meditation and the benefits it would bring me, I decided to have faith that she knew what she was talking about and that it might feel good to explore spirituality. Even though I had read various books on spirituality before, I had never really delved into the study of it because I was too busy raising kids, and running businesses, and pleasing everyone.

Law of Attraction Principle

Since we are an action-oriented society, having faith that everything will work out despite not knowing how to make it happen is one of the hardest concepts to understand. The only way to prove the value of this concept to ourselves is to practice letting go of knowing how and then seeing if things work out. Needing to control the outcome is a low-frequency energy. Having faith (high-frequency energy), on the other hand, allows us to rendezvous with the cooperative components that will bring us our desired results.

While waiting for the month to pass before the meditation class was to start, I began searching TV channels and books that were popular at that time and I happened across Joel Osteen, the well-known author and senior pastor of Lakewood Church in Texas. He'd written his first book, *Your Best Life Now*, which he was promoting at the end of his TV show. I thought to myself, "Wow, I'd sure like to learn how I could find MY best life now . . . when is that coming?!" So, I ordered the book and began reading it daily. As a result, I started to empower myself. The book was full of true-life stories of real people who had overcome all different kinds of serious difficulties and had eventually become happy. These stories began to fill my mind with hope that I could somehow survive the unbearable pain I was feeling. In fact, this was the first time in my life that I experienced the feeling of faith in the unknown. It was relieving to feel that somehow, I too, like the people in his book, could get through the mess I was in and become happy again.

Law of Attraction Principle

When we do not know how to begin to think better-feeling thoughts, start reading and listening to other people's empowering words. All thoughts, even other people's thoughts, produce energy. The longer we focus on new, uplifting thoughts, the stronger the momentum becomes. This momentum helps us to attract new, improved thoughts that will lead us to a better life.

During the same month in 2004, I also happened to watch a PBS TV program in which Dr. Wayne Dyer was promoting his book, *The Power of Intention*, for a discounted price with a donation to PBS. I was drawn to it, so I ordered the book along with his set of six CDs, and continued to empower myself with knowledge, hope, and inspiration.

On one of his CDs, Wayne Dyer spoke about a self-empowering idea that will help you through any painful experience. He recommended that you pay attention to the way you are talking to yourself about your painful event as well as what words you are using when talking to others. The reason this is important is because the words you use to describe any scenario in your life end up painting a vivid picture in your mind. He said that if your words are negative, it's time to put a new *frame* around this picture you've painted in your mind. (Negative thoughts will attract more negative experiences.)

You do this by choosing new, descriptive, positive words. The words you use are like the frame that an artist chooses to put around his or her picture and all artists know that the frame that surrounds a picture will either enhance or detract from its beauty.

My mom was an artist, so I understood this analogy clearly. I realized that I had been saying to myself, and to my close friends and family, that this was the worst thing that could ever happen to me and that it made me feel like a hopeless loser when it came to relationships. I knew I needed to find a new way to think about what I was going through but couldn't come up with any ideas. I was just too stuck in a rut. In other words, the momentum of my negative way of thinking was so powerful that it made it seem impossible to come up with a more positive way of thinking about my situation. One suggestion Dr. Dyer gave was to describe the situation to myself as a *blessing in disguise*. Somehow, I was drawn to this phrase. I decided I liked the idea of the word *blessing*. *Blessing* was commonly used in many different religions that I had read about throughout my life so spiritually, this felt nice. I knew it certainly had to be *in disguise* as I could not see how anything good was ever going to come out of this painful experience!

Slowly, I began to change my thoughts. When I caught myself saying how horrible everything was, I purposefully changed my words and started saying to myself that it was a *blessing in disguise*. Throughout the entire year of our divorce proceedings, I repeated that phrase over and over to myself.

I now know that this was another clear example of how the Law of Attraction works. You attract the results you receive in life according to the thoughts you are continually and habitually thinking.

The month before the meditation class started, I began having faith and hope that I would somehow get through this divorce without falling apart and I allowed myself to wonder what my future might be like. I remember clearly saying to myself, "If I ever have another man in my life, I want him to be a man of integrity and a spiritual man." I put this nice, happy thought out into the Universe and let it go. Quickly, I went back to my habit of negative thinking, telling myself, "Well, that will never happen, because I hate men!"

Finally, the meditation class arrived, and I went with curiosity and some trepidation. Would this really help me? Could I possibly fail at it? The teacher, Laura, welcomed me with open arms. She had a loving and calm demeanor. There were about ten students: a married couple and some single women and men including myself. At first, I felt uncomfortable with the whole experience. During the two-day event, I found myself crying and confused but occasionally experiencing peace and moments of quietness in my mind. When the class was over, Laura mentioned to me that any student who had been through her classes could attend occasional evenings of meditation which she held in her home once every month or so. She invited me to take advantage of this opportunity, so I could continue to practice mediation in a group setting. Building new habits takes practice, time, and focus. Since it was a nice short drive and I appreciated the support she was offering me, I decided to go.

Even though I did not know what was in store for me, the cooperative component that the Universe lined up for me was Laura, who had offered me the opportunity to keep practicing meditation. The vibrational possibilities were in the future, but I first had to allow myself the chance to start raising my vibration, so I could eventually receive what the Universe had in store for me.

Law of Attraction Principle

The Universe continually lines up vibrational possibilities for us to achieve our dreams and desires. I like to call these possibilities, cooperative components in the manifestation process. The vibrational possibilities to what we want are always found in the high-frequency energy field where all good-feeling thoughts, ideas, and solutions exist. When we are thinking negative thoughts that produce a lower frequency, such as doubt, worry, or fear, we will not be able to see or rendezvous with the cooperative components being presented to us. They are invisible to us because we can only rendezvous with experiences that match the frequencies we are emanating. Shifting our vibration to a higher frequency allows us to rendezvous with the cooperative components that will lead us to our desires. This is how we use the Law of Attraction for leverage to receive what we want.

My Knight in Shining Armor Arrives

Okay, he wasn't a knight, he wasn't wearing armor, and there was no spotlight shining on him that singled him out for me, but to my surprise, he ended up being the gift that the Universe had waiting for me. My life expanded in a beautiful way when Laura offered the follow-up meditation classes. I was in such a state of stress and worry that I was unable to see the gift the Universe had waiting for me. Sitting right there in that meditation class was a quiet, peaceful, and spiritual man of integrity named Kevin. The answer to my simple request to the Universe a month earlier was there! That class was my introduction to Kevin; my love, my partner, and my husband-to-be.

At the time, however, I was in such a state of fear and confusion that I did not recognize this gift. I was hating men and just starting my divorce, so I didn't look twice at Kevin. However, because I was willing to continue to learn and grow, the class gave me the opportunity to get to know him during these evenings of meditation. Over the next year, Kevin and I became spiritual friends, just as I'd requested. When the divorce was finalized, I was very thankful that Tiffany James had referred me to my attorney, who had referred me to a meditation class, which had included the hidden gift of a spiritual partner who was to come into my life. This is an ideal example of how the Universe lines up all the cooperative components that you are asking for without you even being aware of it. If you allow yourself to continue to have hope and faith and feel good, you'll finally see your desired manifestation in front of you. Others call this good luck, but I have learned that it is the Law of Attraction in action.

My divorce from Jason was finalized in May 2005 and I was free at last to begin searching for my new life. At this point, my children were grown and on their own and I was totally alone in my home. I could have chosen to feel sorry for myself and live in the "Oh poor me, I'm a victim" mentality but I was happy that I no longer had to worry about pleasing anyone but myself. I was happy to be done running the family-owned business where I had received constant criticism from Jason and that I no longer had to worry about his family's concerns as to what would happen to the business after I left. I began to think only about myself and my personal growth. I began to address what I really wanted to do with the rest of my life. Finally, I was no longer caught in others' struggles and demands.

The choices I made each day finally affected only myself. For someone like me who had been the people-pleasing and nurturing caregiver to four children and two husbands for decades, the freedom to please only myself was exhilarating. When you are at the end of any relationship, I highly recommend living alone for a predetermined length of time and taking the opportunity to learn about yourself. Learn what your true values and desires are and what kind of life you would like to live from that point on. The only relationship that ever needs to be truly understood, experienced, and enhanced is your relationship with yourself.

Choose Your Thoughts Wisely

If you are entering a phase of your life where you want to discover who you really are, I recommend that each day upon waking, you straightaway think about things that make you feel good. Pick something easy, like your beloved dog or cat, or the warm flannel blankets on your bed in winter. Keep it simple and make sure the thought really makes you smile inside. Focus on this great feeling for a few minutes and see what other good-feeling thoughts come to mind. As you repeat this process, momentum will begin to take over. Before your day begins, you will have established a high-frequency, good-feeling state of being. This prepares a vibrational atmosphere around you that will bring the next cooperative component into your day in the form of a thought, a delightful experience, or surprising opportunity. This is how you can ensure that each day is a successful day. Success is as simple as feeling happy all day long!

Law of Attraction Principle

In order to move towards the life that we want and deserve, the most important thing we can do is to keep our focus more on thoughts that feel good than don't. When we do this, we will begin to see how the power of momentum in high-frequency states brings us all that we want.

After my divorce was finalized and I no longer had to focus on the negative energy that divorce always includes. I started being drawn to doing only things that felt good to me.

I love music and when I lived with Jason, we always listened to country music – and no wonder: it's so often full of drama! On the first day alone in my house, without Jason around to make negative comments about my musical choices, I realized that I could listen to something other than country music. I turned on my favorite upbeat Whitney Houston songs and happily began cleaning my whole house, singing my lungs out.

I decided to change the look of my bedroom to a new, sweet feminine look. I treated myself to vases full of beautiful flowers, brand new sheets, a comforter, and a warm, soft, king-sized down-filled pillow to hug. When I was done transforming my space, I started dancing along to my happy music with my dog Roxie. She romped around the house with me and I could swear she was smiling the whole time. It may sound funny to dance with your dog, but it was great to share my feeling of freedom and joy in that moment with her.

Another thing that I found fun but had never allowed myself to do was walking around the house naked without worrying about what anyone else thought. Oh yes, I did have all the drapes closed! It was time to go ahead and look in the mirror, smile, and begin to love myself unconditionally. (Try it – it's liberating!)

It was so much fun to select only the TV shows that I wanted to watch. No more of the sports, negative news, or politically-focused programs that Jason always insisted on watching as soon as he walked into the house.

Law of Attraction Principle

Everything is energy. The thoughts and sounds coming from our TV set, radio, CDs, movies, and all communication happening on social media produce energy that influences the atmosphere in which we're living.

Jason could not stand silence in the house. To avoid this, he constantly had the TV turned to negative news channels and political programs whose controversial topics always irritated me. I tried to tune them out, but I couldn't. Even if you think you are tuning something out, you're just ignoring the truth and pretending that it's all right. You are lying to yourself and the truth is that everything is not okay.

Once Jason was gone, I started recording my favorite shows. I recorded Joel Osteen's program every Sunday morning on NBC and National Geographic programs about nature. I recorded shows that were funny, inspiring, and positive, along with shows that were educational, such as documentaries and biographies of successful and happy people. When I wanted to sit down and relax or lift my spirits, I had plenty of recordings to choose from. Whatever I happened to be drawn to, I watched.

I highly recommend searching through the Oprah Winfrey Network (OWN) as you can find some great programming there. My favorites are Oprah Winfrey', *Super Soul Sunday,* and, *Oprah's Master Class.* They are always uplifting. Oprah interviews many people who have overcome difficult, and even tragic, situations and have ended up happy and fulfilled. These programs are great reminders that you are not alone and that you too can overcome anything if you want to!

When you are going through a difficult transition, whether divorce or any other serious life-changing event, I highly recommend that you continually fill your mind with positive and uplifting programs, books and/or CDs. You can also find uplifting things for free at your local library and on YouTube. Select a topic and go for it. If it feels negative in any way, stop reading or listening to it and find something else. Abraham-Hicks YouTube clips are great for helping you to understand how to use the Law of Attraction effectively and the TED Talks include many inspiring topics. I also feel it is worth recording your favorite TV programs because then you will never inadvertently expose yourself to negative programs again! When you choose empowering things to read and listen to, it helps you to move your own personal vibration up to a good-feeling place. The Law of Attraction will then bring you more ideas and experiences that feel good, to help you move forward in your life and realize your true desires. I know this because it has worked for me and for many other women that I've coached.

I love being outdoors and as the divorce was finalized in May, and spring had arrived in Michigan, I started walking Roxie daily while listening to my favorite music. I began to love picking the foods I wanted to eat and cooking only for myself and enjoyed not having to think about keeping anyone else's favorite foods in the house. I started eating less and was drawn to healthier food choices and eventually I even began jogging with Roxie. As a bonus, at the age of 58, the advantage of making all those inspired choices helped me to get into the best physical shape I had been in for years.

Law of Attraction Principle

Action steps are only beneficial when we are *inspired* to act, that is, wanting to do something from our heart. If we instead act from the idea of *Motivation*, which includes pushing hard, working twenty-four/seven, or taking the "no pain, no gain" approach, however, we will slow our desired manifestation from showing up. This is because all those approaches come from a place of negative energy. *Motivation* pushes us to work hard to get the prize at the end whereas *Inspiration* pulls us forward into action because it comes from the true desires in our heart.

When my new life began, I decided that I never wanted to work in an office for anyone else again, so I happily set about rebuilding my UndercoverWear business. I was excited that in the first year after my divorce, UndercoverWear was offering two opportunities to earn all-expenses-paid trips – a week in Hawaii and a week in Punta Cana in the Dominican Republic. UndercoverWear trip opportunities always inspired me to act so this was a great time for me to really enjoy focusing on rebuilding my deteriorating business and earn two free trips as a bonus! I knew how to earn trips with UndercoverWear as I had accomplished it every year of my career, even throughout my difficult marriages with George and Jason. As such, I jumped right in and called everyone I knew to build up my booking schedule which had fallen to about one party a week in the last few years. I filled my calendar with lots of bookings. How? I was happy! And since I was no longer feeling forced to do anything, I was inspired to act. It felt so good!

When you are happy, you're drawn to taking inspired action steps and the Law of Attraction always brings you the results you want. For me, it meant a busy booking schedule, which brought me security in the form of money to support myself and points toward earning those two trips.

I continued to read inspiring authors' books and to listen to their CDs, especially Wayne Dyer and Louise Hay. I also began to make sure I attended Laura's follow-up meditation gatherings. Kevin had also decided to continue to attend these meditation events and this allowed us to get to know each other little by little.

PART FIVE:

Stepping Into My Life of Joy

My Personal Journey of Self-Discovery Begins

In 2005, Kevin and I began to talk on the phone in the evenings and I was really drawn to his kind words of wisdom and the comforting sound of his voice. He knew I was focusing on rebuilding my UndercoverWear business and suggested that I join the networking group he was involved with. He said he had gotten many new clients for his computer business by participating in his chapter and maybe it would do the same for me. I had never done any kind of networking before as I'd always gotten my bookings from shows but since I respected Kevin so much, I decided to check out one of his chapter's meetings.

I know now that the Universe had lined up another cooperative component for me that day. I have always been inspired by powerful speakers and it just so happened that at this meeting, the main speaker was a person who had been a motivational speaker in his earlier career. If he had been a low-key, boring speaker, I wouldn't have been intrigued at the idea of belonging to a business networking organization but since he was so dynamic, I decided to give it a try. And even though I wasn't sure how I would get lingerie parties from a group of thirty or so mostly-male business owners, I decided to join the chapter anyway.

Many good things happened after I made that decision. Universal possibilities that I wasn't expecting started lining up for me. These included building rewarding, new relationships, learning how to trust that I don't have to do everything alone, and that others (especially men) are available to help and support me when I allow them. After a few months of getting to know everyone in the chapter, I did start to receive some bookings. After all, men do like lingerie, and they do have women in their lives! In addition, the organization provided excellent training and I learned how to become an effective networker. Every week each member presented a one-minute commercial about their business and I found that this helped me to continually speak about all the benefits of UndercoverWear over other party-plan companies. It helped me to keep focused on my career in a positive way. It also felt good to learn about, and to be able to recommend, the various services and products of the other business owners whom I'd come to know and trust.

The other benefit that I hadn't expected was that I would be seeing Kevin each week at the networking meetings. This caused our friendship to expand in a new way. I came to really respect him as a business owner and, after the meetings, we often went for coffee and continued talking about our businesses and how all of us in our group could help each other. By the summer of 2006, Kevin and I had a very comfortable friendship.

On one sunny Saturday in June, our networking group was hosting a fun social afternoon of Whirlyball which involves dividing up into teams of five and riding around on a basketball court in big bumper cars. Each player holds a whiffle racket and a hard, plastic whiffle ball is hit back and forth until it is tossed into the net to score. I had never played before and wasn't planning on going as it sounded like something that mostly men would like to do. Kevin convinced me to go by reminding me that I might get some bookings as all the wives were invited, too. I liked the idea of meeting more ladies as potential UndercoverWear hostesses, so I decided to go.

My relationship with Kevin began to evolve that day. For the first time since I had met him, we enjoyed a lot of laughter and fun together, in contrast to the meditation and business experiences we had shared up until then. I noticed that he only had one beer throughout the whole afternoon of fun and I was impressed because both of my ex-husbands would have had many drinks over those few hours.

After the event was over, Kevin asked me if I would like to go sit in a park and enjoy the remaining hours of the beautiful, warm, sunny summer afternoon. It sounded nice and we ended up going to a park close to his home and sitting on a blanket under a big beautiful tree and relaxing together. We had so much in common and found that talking together was easy. Time flew by and before we knew it, the moon was coming up and the stars were shining brightly. Finally, I said, "I guess it's time to go," and we touched hands. At that moment, I felt a powerful spark of energy run up my arm and down my back that tingled so beautifully! I'd never experienced this feeling in my whole life. It felt so good that it scared me a little bit. Was it love? Was it lust? I didn't know but I worried that I wasn't ready for either.

He said, "Yes, I suppose we should get going, but if you want, I live just around the corner, and you're welcome to come over. I do have something I'd like to show you." I didn't want the evening to end so we went to his house.

I felt so comfortable entering his home! It was clean, organized, and so inviting. We sat on the couch and continued talking. He made us a small healthy dinner of shrimp and fruit and we watched some of his favorite shows that he'd recorded. Eventually, he remembered that he wanted to show me something, went up to his bedroom and came down with a photo album that he'd put together during his teen years. He shared with me some of his personal memories of important events that he had experienced and captured in pictures. I was honored that he trusted me enough to share his private memories, dreams, and desires with me. The evening was so warm and relaxing, and every time he gently touched my back or put his arm around me, I felt that beautiful energy run through my body. When the evening was over, we hugged and kissed, and I had an overwhelming feeling of being at home and safe in the arms of a wonderful man. This was another first for me!

We continued to talk on the phone almost every evening after that. I really enjoyed the sound of his soothing voice and found it a perfect way to end my day. During one of our many discussions, Kevin confided to me that when he started his own computer business, he'd been so uncomfortable talking with strangers that he worried about how he would ever be able to talk to people and find new clients. A good friend had recommended that he take a Dale Carnegie course to help him get over his fear of public speaking, so he bought Dale Carnegie's book, *How to Win Friends and Influence People.* He read it seven times before he found the courage to enroll in the twelve-week program.

Week after week, his confidence had begun to build, and, by the end of the course, it had changed his life. He'd not only overcome his fear – he had realized that he loved helping others step out of their comfort zones and overcome their own fears. After sharing this with me, he suggested that I might want to take that course. Honestly, I felt confident talking in front of people after all the years of experience I'd had in UndercoverWear, so I wasn't sure if this was something I needed. He said that each Carnegie student also learns thirty human relations principles that are very empowering, and the experience ends up providing a personal journey of self-discovery for everyone who participates. This caught my attention because even though I was a confident speaker, I knew deep down inside when it came to relationships, I had some personal growth I needed to go through before I could ever think of having another man in my life.

Moving Forward

Since I'd already gone through two failed marriages, a personal journey of self-discovery sounded intriguing, so I signed up for the twelve-week program in the fall of 2006. Each Dale Carnegie instructor would ask a few volunteers who had graduated from a previous Dale Carnegie course to assist by coaching students who needed help and support with preparing their weekly two-minute talk. Kevin had done this before so, to support me as a good friend, he decided he would volunteer once again as a coach in the class for which I had registered.

Each week we learned so many wonderful ways to communicate effectively and I was enjoying learning all the human relations principles, some of which I already knew and had been using, and some I hadn't. We went home each week with a new topic for a speech to prepare for the next week's class. Most students are nervous and fearful, but the instructor and coaches were always very positive and supportive. Each one would get up and give their own two-minute talk on a topic from their own life experience to set an example for the students.

I am happy to say that taking the Dale Carnegie Course changed my life as well! I had no idea that I would learn so much about myself and about how communication affects every one of my relationships, both at work and at home. I learned that during any form of communication, the different choices of words, brought on different emotional responses and different results. When we chose words that felt good to us, like appreciation and encouragement, we would receive a positive result with the person or group we were communicating with and when we used words that felt bad such as judgment or criticism, we would receive negative results.

Experiencing this program with Kevin as a coach allowed us to become closer friends. Each week we would talk about subjects that wouldn't have come up in everyday conversation and our friendship continued to strengthen. We discussed defining moments in our childhood and many other personal topics. Each week, as Kevin gave his two-minute talk, he revealed new aspects of his personality and life journey that I wouldn't have otherwise known about.

One week, about halfway through the course, we were given an assignment to prepare a two-minute talk about something that made us angry. It threw me off guard. Every week, I would happily go home and enjoy preparing for the following weeks' two-minute talk. This assignment really bothered me though and I told the instructor that I did not want to do it because I'd lived many long years with verbally abusive and angry men, and I considered anger a childish and immature emotion. I simply refused to do it. The instructor was very nice and told me she understood how I felt and that all that she expected of me was to come to class and watch. That evening as Kevin drove me home, I told him that I did not want to participate. He was just as supportive as the instructor had been. He asked me not to worry about it but to plan to attend anyway and just observe the others giving their talks. So, with no pressure from anyone, I agreed.

When the next week arrived, Kevin picked me up and we drove there together as we'd done for the previous six weeks. I sat way in the back of the class and continued to profess that I was not going to participate but was willing to watch. As always, the coaches were called to the front to give their examples of the talk before we gave ours. When Kevin's turn came, I was intrigued and curious as I had never seen him angry in the two years I'd known him. In fact, I didn't think he had a mean bone in his body. At that point in our relationship we had spent a lot of time together meditating, talking, laughing, working at our businesses, and having fun, but we had never shared any negative feelings, such as anger, with each other.

So that evening, after learning some more about human relations principles, the time came to do the talk on something that bothers us. The instructor called Kevin to the front of the room and all the students were eager to see the first demonstration of how to do this talk. The instructor asked him to stand in front of the class behind a table and read a few sentences that were written on a whiteboard, the purpose of which was to get the angry feelings started. She also gave Kevin a silly-looking, skinny rubber chicken to hold in his hand which had two long legs that made it very easy to grip.

As Kevin began to read the phrase, his voice began to rise and he began to beat the chicken on the table in front of him as the instructor had asked him to. Within a minute, he had allowed himself to get animated and finally yelled out: "You know what makes me angry?" The students yelled back, "What?" and he yelled, "Parents who verbally abuse their children!" The students eagerly responded yelling "YES, YES, YES! We agree!" In two minutes, the room was full of supportive energy.

Suddenly, it was over, and the teacher was thanking Kevin for his willingness to share an example of what this short talk could look like. The anger was completely gone, and everyone was feeling better.

I must admit I was totally impressed as I had never seen him this way. It scared me for a minute because it reminded me of my two past husbands yelling at me. But then, I became inspired and thought to myself, "Well, if sweet, kind, gentle Kevin can do this, why can't I?" I waited in the back row as each of the forty students gave their talk. Finally, as the last remaining student, I decided to give it a try, reminding myself that if Kevin could do it, so could I.

I hadn't planned a subject at all and had no idea what I was going to say but I went up to the front of the room anyway, picked up the chicken, and began to read the phrase to build up some feelings of anger. Within the short, few seconds that it took to read the phrase, what I was going to say popped into my head. I began beating the chicken on the table with a lot of enthusiasm and began to scream at the top of my lungs, "You know what makes me angry? I hate liars!" The students cheered along with me "Yes! Yes! Yes!" Then I said, "You know what else I hate? I hate people who cheat on their spouses!" By this point, I was seriously screaming and shaking with anger and beating the hell out of the chicken to the point of almost breaking off its head! The students were all supportive and cheering me on. The time flew by and the instructor gently came over to me, put her hands on my shoulders and said in a sweet tone, "That was very good, Suzanne. You can sit down now."

I went to the back of the room, shaking like a leaf with a few tears running down my cheeks. Kevin came over and gave me a supportive hug and said, "You did a very good job!" He was proud that I had decided to step out of my comfort zone and give it a try. I must admit that I was too. When the teacher asked what any of us had learned from this talk, I raised my hand. I shared, "I feel like I've lost ten pounds without even going on a diet. It's like the weight of the world has been lifted off my shoulders!"

Before this experience, I didn't know the value in allowing myself to feel anger and release it on purpose, so this experience became a defining moment for me. When I look back on it now, I realize that in all the years of participating in verbal abuse, I had never let myself feel true anger to the depths of the experience in Dale Carnegie. Choosing to see myself as a victim, I'd easily go into depression which made me feel like a loser. By habit, the way I'd move from this sad state into feeling better was when I'd turn my focus to my UndercoverWear business. This temporarily helped me feel happy while ignoring the pain of my relationships. This is a method of distraction and it does help in the moment but it's not a long-term solution.

Law of Attraction Principle

When we're feeling bad, emotional relief is always a thought away. Temporarily changing our thoughts from the bad-feeling situation at hand by refocusing on a different but better-feeling situation is one way of using the Law of Attraction for leverage. This will temporarily help us get though the day. This is called *the distraction method.*

Keep in mind that the power of momentum holds us firmly in whatever emotional state (good or bad) we are in. Every emotion is important to acknowledge because it's telling us what to expect next. When we look at the emotional scale chart shown in the preface of this book, we can see that, when we're feeling depressed or powerless, the only way up is to move into anger. Any emotion that feels a little bit better than hopelessness is an improvement and a sign that you are raising your frequency. Think of it as if we are taking ourselves by the hand and walking ourselves up the emotional scale, just like a supportive parent takes our hand as we learn to walk up a set of stairs as a young child. Instead of taking steps we are choosing new thoughts that begin to help us find some relief, one thought at a time. Just as no one can climb a set of stairs in only one step, no one can think themselves from a state of depression up to a state of joy instantly. We can, however, learn how to gradually think supportive little thoughts to ourselves that will move us, one thought at a time, into higher vibrational states until we eventually feel better. This self-empowering technique allows us to raise our frequency so that we can begin to receive better feeling experiences via Law of Attraction.

Law of Attraction Principle

When we're in depression, fear, and powerlessness, the way to move out of it is to think thoughts that will bring us relief. As we choose thoughts that help us release negative energy, we empower ourselves with the truth of where we are at which helps us move towards where we want to be. This is called, *walking up the emotional scale.*

Although the distraction method helped me to feel better in the moment, I came to realize that simply distracting myself at times was not enough to change my long-term vibration around men which subsequently prevented me from attracting enjoyable relationships. My thoughts about relationships were still self-defeating and so I hadn't yet realized that, if you keep on thinking what you've been thinking, you'll keep on getting what you've been getting.

Law of Attraction Principle

If we want to stop a cycle of misery, we must begin by recognizing the thought patterns that relate to the subject or area of life in which we want improvement. We do this by allowing ourselves to feel the emotions around these thought patterns, no matter how painful they might be. It's only when we allow ourselves to feel the feelings that those thought patterns are creating that we then have the power to choose better-feeling ones.

For example, I used to think I had bad luck when it came to men. I got down on myself and concluded that I must be a real loser since I'd never experienced a good relationship in either of my marriages. My parents had been great role models and were loving and respectful of each other. They made marriage look so easy that I thought I must be doing something wrong. Why couldn't I please the men I'd married? Why did they both lie to me and have affairs and drink? I certainly felt that I had tried everything possible to make them happy and yet they both accused me of being too fat, and in their eyes, unworthy of their loyalty.

My self-esteem was very low after divorcing George and since I didn't feel good about myself when it came to relationships, the Law of Attraction brought me Jason, another man with low self-esteem. How do I know that both my husbands had low self-esteem? In the beginning of each relationship, they had both told me that their parents never considered them good enough. When children hear judgmental words and are constantly criticized by their parents, their self-esteem plummets. Most parents don't realize the impact this has on their children, but the result is usually that the children end up feeling bad about themselves. On the other hand, children who do *not* receive verbal abuse from their parents are much more likely to feel confident about themselves because they live in a higher-frequency state of being. As a result, these children only attract others having high self-esteem.

To stop a cycle of misery, self-examination of our thought patterns and how we acquired them can be a good place to begin. This is the time to speak the truth to ourselves and acknowledge the habit of thought that has not served us. This is where allowing ourselves to feel *all* our emotions and feel them deeply is essential. When I did this for myself, the emotions of hopelessness, unworthiness, and anger showed up. We can't change what we aren't aware of and we can't release an emotion that we haven't acknowledged. The Law of Attraction always reflects back to us experiences that will show us our buried emotions until it finally gets our attention, so we can change them.

I am thankful that the Law of Attraction lined up my experience in Dale Carnegie. We always have choices and because I chose to participate in the talk on anger it became a turning point for me. Once I let those angry feelings come out, my life began to improve in wonderful ways. That pent-up, negative energy I had held and ignored for so long was finally released and I was free to begin attracting more of the good things I wanted into my life.

Integrity

Because I had chosen to take the Dale Carnegie course, Kevin and I were seeing each other twice a week. At that point, I began to fall in love with him. One evening, after a very sexually passionate time together, I remember saying, "I love you". Kevin didn't say "I love you" back but he hugged me warmly and later explained to me that, "Yes, our relationship is fantastic and all of it has been amazing, but I never say the word 'love' until I really mean it." I was disappointed at first and thought to myself that I would never allow myself to become vulnerable again in that way. After thinking about it carefully, however, I began to respect him even more.

Integrity was a characteristic that I knew I wanted in a man and I certainly did not want someone saying something they didn't really mean.

I continued to love Kevin, expressing it in many ways, and decided that I just wouldn't say the word "love" again. I admired so many things about him and I knew I wanted him in my life as a wonderful friend for as long as it felt right for both of us. Being aware that I was thirteen years older than he was, I decided that keeping him as a friend until he found someone just right for him would still be okay with me. I'd also become aware that it was much more fun to live in the present and not spend time worrying about the future because no one knows how long that will be anyway. I was feeling great about my life! I loved everything I was learning about myself and I enjoyed being independent and making all my decisions based on what I wanted to do. I loved letting go of all the people-pleasing habits I had acquired over the years and figured that my friendship with Kevin was so strong that it would continue even if he found someone else his own age. Allowing myself to be true to me and allowing him to explore his own desires seemed perfect. If you ever want a great relationship, allowing each other to be exactly who you are is the key. Unconditional love works all the time, every time!

Life is About Having Fun

I was very busy in the first year after the divorce as I began rebuilding my UndercoverWear career. I was excited about setting my own schedule and being my own boss and I was happily doing many parties and recruiting women onto my team. On the nights that I was doing parties on Kevin's side of town, I would stop in and see him after the show and sometimes even have the pleasure of spending the night there – more fun! I was thrilled that I ended up qualifying for both of UndercoverWear's week-long, all-expenses-paid trips to Hawaii and to the Dominican Republic.

Both of my sisters had been very supportive throughout my miserable and stressful divorces. I asked Linda if she would like to be my guest on the free trip to Hawaii that I had earned, since my sister Kathy and her husband had already traveled there. I was so appreciative of the fact that I was single and could ask anyone I wanted to travel with me. I was also happy that I would no longer be embarrassed by alcoholic husbands while on vacation. Of course, Linda said yes, and I was very thankful that she could get vacation time off from work to join me. We had so much fun! I'll always look back on our vacation together as the best way I could have celebrated the beginning of my new life.

After Hawaii, the next six months flew by and before I knew it, the trip to Punta Cana was coming up. Kevin had been such a good friend for three years and everything we'd shared together had been so rewarding; I knew in my heart that I really wanted to invite him to join me on this trip. I loved him, and he, occasionally, had been saying that he loved me, too! I knew there was no one else I would rather take on this trip. I had originally planned to take Linda but when I discussed it with her, she was very understanding. She was happy that I had found a man so different from my previous husbands to enjoy my life with.

Law of Attraction Principle

When we love and respect ourselves, we then can attract others who love and respect as well.

Life is like a mirror: the experiences we are having are always an exact reflection of the thought energy we're emitting. Before Kevin, the men in my life did not respect me. In hindsight, I can see that deep down inside I did not like or respect myself. When I began to understand and practice the Law of Attraction, I stopped all my self-criticism and started loving myself just the way I am. One of the things I always admired about Kevin was how much respect he showed me. I didn't put it all together until later, but from the very beginning of our relationship and every single day since then, Kevin would make sure he walked with me to my side of the car and open and close the door for me. It may be hard to believe but I had never experienced this before! I'd seen my dad doing it for my mom all the time but by the time I was married, I didn't even think about anyone showing me this kind of respect. Because I had such a habit of doing everything on my own, it took several times for me to accept his respect and to see the value of allowing him to treat me in this kind manner. When I asked Kevin if he would like to join me on a vacation in the Dominican Republic, he was a little more hesitant than my sister to accept my invitation. It would be a free trip for him and he did not want to take advantage of me. He felt he should be paying some portion of the expenses, but I assured him that it wasn't necessary since I'd earned it and it was totally free for me. I was thrilled when, after a week of serious thought, he finally accepted my invitation!

Enjoying a vacation in the tropics in the middle of a long, cold Michigan winter was such a pleasure. It was January of 2007 when we arrived at the resort in Punta Cana and the weather was beautiful. At the mature and beautiful age of nearly 60, it was the most romantic vacation I had ever experienced in my life. We kayaked, rented WaveRunners and enjoyed massages in the spa at the resort. We walked on the beach and enjoyed the warmth of the sun each day. When we'd had enough of the beach, we found comfortable chairs to lounge on out by the pool. Kevin enjoyed lying under the shade of a palm tree with me lying next to him, soaking up all the sun I could get. It was perfect. When I would get hot, we'd hop into the pool and Kevin would gently pull me around in the refreshing water. When night arrived, we'd walk along the beach, watch the beautiful sunset, and talk about life.

One evening, cuddling on lounge chairs out by the water, we gazed out over the moonlit ocean. The tropical breeze was warm and refreshing and as we relaxed and looked up, thousands of stars lit up the sky. With no Detroit city lights to obstruct our view, the vastness of this amazing universe could clearly be seen. We talked about our dreams, our goals, and our desires. We seemed to be on the same wavelength about everything. It was heartwarming and magnificent and will be etched in my memory forever.

Surprise!

The final day of our vacation arrived. We wanted our last meal to be special, so we decided to find a table all to ourselves at one of the many restaurants in the resort. I'd been happier on this vacation than I'd ever been before, and I really didn't want it to come to an end.

After we ordered our meal, Kevin gently reached across the table, took my hand and looked into my eyes. As we touched, I felt genuine warmth and love coming from him. I looked back into his beautiful blue eyes and he paused for a moment. He took a deep breath and began to tell me how sincerely and deeply he loved me. Much to my amazement, during this unforgettable and tender moment, he asked me to marry him!

Having just experienced the most romantic week I'd ever had in my life; my heart was bursting with joy. I continued to hold Kevin's hand and looked deep into his eyes and thought about how lucky I was to have found such a sweet, gentle soul to spend the rest of my life with. Soft tears of joy began to fall down my cheeks. I was on cloud nine! It seemed like my own personal fairy tale had come true.

Up until that moment, I had become completely at peace with the idea that Kevin and I would *just* be friends forever. I was totally surprised when I heard his gentle, loving voice ask me to be his wife. Instantly, I knew how I truly felt, and I happily said, "Yes!"

Two years had gone by since my second divorce was final, and throughout that time, I had been learning how to respect myself, be true to myself, and most importantly, love myself unconditionally. In hindsight, I realize that the Law of Attraction could not have brought Kevin and me together if I had not changed my old belief patterns and the way I was thinking about myself. Since like attracts like, I had become the kind of person I wanted to attract as a partner and so the Universe couldn't help but bring us together!

Fairytales really can have a happy ending.

Epilogue

Since the day Kevin asked me to marry him, our love story has been continually expanding. In 2007, Kevin and I started our own intuitive coaching company called, Personal Success Programs LLC. We assist clients in moving through blocks, building self-awareness, and expanding their self-empowerment so they can step more fully into the lives they want and deserve.

Throughout our 14 years of friendship and 11 years of marriage, we have deepened our understanding of the Law of Attraction to create an amazing life together. Although we've manifested both joyful and painful experiences together, throughout it all, having this understanding has helped us own our part in each attraction, allowing our love and respect for each other to deepen as well.

In the fall of 2014, a series of events happened that made me question my understanding of the Law of Attraction. My youngest son was diagnosed with cancer. It continued to reoccur over the next year with several more surgeries that followed. During this time, our family experienced the loss of a sweet, happy 7-month-old great-grandbaby through SIDS (sudden infant death syndrome) and 4 weeks later, my beautiful 35-year old niece left this world through suicide. I found myself asking "why is this happening?"

I wondered what more I needed to learn, and I intuitively started searching for answers that might shed some light on the complexities of how life works. I continued to listen to more Abraham-Hicks videos and then I discovered Teal Swan, Bruce Lipton, Gregg Braden, and Jessica Alstrom. These teachings helped me understand the Law of Attraction more fully and the value of uncovering and releasing my own hidden childhood shadows. I learned that the energy of our thoughts and the beliefs we've developed in childhood become imbedded in our cellular memory. It may be easier to think that these childhood beliefs, unbeknownst to us, are buried in our subconscious. These emotional memories need to be acknowledged and released so they don't attract (by default) situations that mirror this unconscious, stuck negative energy.

Law of Attraction Principle

The stuck energy of our own negative, self-defeating childhood thoughts remains within us and will continue to attract unwanted (low-frequency) experiences until the manifestations get painful enough to catch our attention. Becoming aware of them and letting go of these beliefs is an important step in manifesting a happier life.

Most of us have grown up in a society that forces us to repress our inner child. With the new information I'd been learning since publishing my first edition, I began to understand myself better. It became clear to me why I had continued to attract some things I didn't want even after I married the love of my life and soulmate, Kevin. I began to examine my thoughts and feelings of the past. I was thankful I had released a lot of anger via my Dale Carnegie experience, however, there are many more emotions than just anger so I knew there must be more for me to explore.

In the fall of 2015, two things happened simultaneously that made me feel anxious and fearful. Our income dropped dramatically because Kevin ended his IT career and my son went through his 4th surgery to remove more cancer. During this stressful time, I had been thinking, "isn't there more that I could do to help our finances and also help with the situation regarding my son's health?" I decided to sit quietly and become mindful. I decided to focus on my emotions of fear and helplessness to see what I might learn about myself. In both situations I subconsciously went back to an old, self-defeating habit of thought that *I wasn't good enough* to have a happy life.

I used a combination of techniques from Teal Swan's, *Completion Process,* along with Jessica Alstrom's, *Becoming the Real You,* that helped me work through these old habits.

I began to review my childhood and remembered when I first felt that I needed to do more to be considered worthy. As the painful emotion of unworthiness arose within me, I let myself feel it fully.

A pattern started to reveal itself to me. In the past, I used to think that if I had tried harder to please the men in my life, my marriages would have been saved and I would have been happy. I also realized that this feeling had also occurred when I pressured myself to achieve all A's in school to please my dad.

I continued to sit in stillness with the feeling of unworthiness and eventually realized that this feeling of not being good enough may have started when my mother put me on a diet (mentioned earlier in the chapter titled Hating Myself). At that time in my life, as a young child, I felt alone and sad because I did not understand why I was the only one in my family who had to go on a diet. In my innocent child's mind, I decided *I must not be good enough* to belong in my family. I sat quietly and felt the deep pain of my broken heart as a young child. I cried hard for a few minutes. I took a deep breath and looked at this painful memory in my mind from the viewpoint of my current broader adult perspective. In my mind, I gave my child-like image of myself a big loving, nurturing hug and reminded myself from this point on, I will always be there for me.

As I comforted myself, a feeling of relief surfaced. I became aware that I no longer had to feel like I wasn't good enough because that wasn't the truth but just something that my child's mind had conjured up. Within about 5 minutes, I had released the negative energy of a buried false childhood belief I'd burdened myself with for most of my life. I was pleased that it didn't take years of therapy but only my willingness to go deep within, be honest with myself, move into the fearful emotion, and love myself to neutralize the fear. When we're stuck in a vicious cycle of pain, facing into our pain and moving through it dissipates its hold over us.

I'm constantly reminded that when it comes to the Law of Attraction, the bottom line is, the universe always answers *yes*. That is, it's always reflecting back to me the essence of what I'm sending out, regardless of whether I'm aware of what I'm sending out or not. Thus, the most important thing I've learned above all else is to become aware of what I'm sending out and I do this by tuning into my feelings. This one simple truth is what's allowed me to transform my life and create the life of joy I now have!

Appendix

Law of Attraction in a Nutshell

Energy

According to physics, everything is energy. The Law of Attraction states that energy vibrating at the same frequency always coalesces or comes together. *Simply stated, like energy attracts like energy.* As such:

- Each thought is a burst of energy that vibrates at a certain frequency.
- Each thought frequency produces a different emotion within us (solar plexus).
- Our emotions let us know what frequency we're sending out into the universe.
- *Good-feeling* thoughts and emotions produce high vibrating frequencies.
- *Bad-feeling* thoughts and emotions produce low vibrating frequencies.

Momentum

One brief thought by itself is not attractive in nature. It has no power because it hasn't had a chance to build up momentum. Thus, there is no need to worry about every little thought we think. A steady stream of thoughts, however, builds up momentum and, over time, becomes more powerful and attractive in nature.

We've all learned about the law of gravity and can easily see how it works. One way to feel how momentum works is to walk down a steep hill. As our descent begins, it's very easy to take steps. Momentum builds the further we walk down the steep hill and the likelihood of falling also increases.

The Law of Attraction is like gravity in that momentum increases its power. Most people don't realize that the longer we focus on something, the stronger the pull is and the more attractive our thoughts become. The book, *Ask and It Is Given,* written by Esther and Jerry Hicks, explains that it only takes seventeen seconds of pure focused thought, having a certain emotion, to build up enough momentum to start the attraction process. More thoughts with the same emotional content are then brought to us. After only sixty-eight seconds of pure, focused thought, the Law of Attraction starts bringing us physical experiences that match the emotional frequency of our ongoing thoughts.

Cooperative Components

Once momentum begins, the Law of Attraction continually lines up cooperative components for us to rendezvous with. First, we rendezvous with more thoughts that reflect the emotion we're feeling. Eventually, as momentum builds, we rendezvous with experiences such as people, places, or things that match our emotion.

For example, in 2004 I was looking for a way to begin to feel better after learning about Jason's double life. One of the first cooperative components the Law of Attraction lined up for me was an introduction to my attorney. The next cooperative component appeared when my attorney suggested I take a meditation class (which is certainly not the average thing an attorney recommends). Another cooperative component was the fact that I got the one remaining space left in the class.

While waiting for the class to begin, the next cooperative component came in the form of Joel Osteen. I had been browsing through the TV channels and just happened to stop on his program. I was inspired and drawn to purchase his book, *Your Best Life Now.* After reading it, I rendezvoused with new emotions I had never felt before. For the first time in my life, I felt the feelings of hope and faith.

I not only began to empower myself with the practice of meditation during my new class, but I also rendezvoused for the first time with Kevin, my future husband. I certainly wasn't looking for a new man in my life. I was just beginning a divorce. I've learned from experience that sometimes you will not recognize a transformative rendezvous in the moment because you're stuck in a rut of stress like I was when I attended the meditation class. I was totally unaware that Kevin, who was also in attendance, would become my husband and soulmate in the next few years.

The cooperative component of ongoing meditation gatherings kept providing more rendezvous with Kevin. These get togethers allowed me to get to know him, feel comfortable with him, and learn how to trust men again. This enabled us to build a comfortable and valuable friendship which became the basis of our marriage.

All the cooperative components and rendezvous eventually led me to my desired outcome which was finding a better life and learning how to feel happy again. Keep in mind that I didn't have a strategic plan for any of these life-changing events. I didn't have a list of things to do nor did I work endless hours trying to find happiness. I just allowed myself to think thoughts that felt better, dream about good feeling possibilities and take life one day at a time. I simply chose to go with the flow and then acted on my impulses. The Universe supported my desires and the Law of Attraction did the rest.

Manifestations

Manifestations that turn into experiences are oftentimes called synchronicities, or coincidences, by people who are not familiar with the Law of Attraction. I have proven to myself that these coincidences are cooperative *components* that we rendezvous with as a result of the Law of Attraction. When synchronicities or coincidences feel good, instead of realizing these are manifestations that we've created, people unfamiliar to the Law of Attraction call them good luck. When things manifest that feel bad, they're often called bad luck.

Here are some examples of what some people call good luck.

- We've been thinking about a person and we *just happen* to run into them.
- It's raining out and we *just happen* to get the front row parking space we wanted.
- We've heard about a new restaurant we want to try, and a good friend *just happens* to call us and invite us to have dinner there.
- We attend an event, and, with perfect timing, we *just happen* to meet someone who has the answer to a question we have or, vice versa, we meet someone at the event who has been searching for help in our area of expertise and we *just happen* to have an answer for them.

Rendezvous

Another way to look at the Law of Attraction is to think of it as the Law of Rendezvous. We're continually being sent a stream of intuitive impulses that line us up with rendezvous equal to the emotions we are feeling. When we're feeling bad, we rendezvous with things we don't want. When we're feeling good, we'll rendezvous with things we do want.

Mirroring

The Law of Attraction can also be called the Law of Mirroring or Law of Reflection. Law of Attraction works like a mirror because it's always reflecting back to us experiences equal to the emotions we're feeling. When we frown into a mirror, it does not reflect a smile back. If we don't like what we are seeing in our life, keep in mind that it is a reflection of the energy we are emitting into the universe. This is often hard to understand because we have been trained in society to ignore or dismiss our emotions. When we attract something we don't want, we think that it's bad luck because we have numbed the emotion within us and don't realize we have attracted it. Many people walk around with a false smile on their faces even though buried inside they feel miserable. This is the way we attract things by default or why life sometimes feels like good luck, bad luck, or potluck. None of us attracts unwanted things on purpose so no need to feel guilty when things show up that we don't want. These unwanted things can actually be clarifying moments that can inspire us to pay attention to our hidden emotions!

Emotional Guidance

The experience we attract will always feel like the same emotion that we were originally having when we attracted it. (Keep in mind we may also be numbing our true emotion at the time when we attract something.) Our emotions are always guiding us so paying attention to our emotions is the KEY to manifesting what we want.

Every goal and every desire we ever have consists of good feeling high frequency thoughts. This is because when we think about our dreams coming true, it feels really good. No one ever wants things that are going to make them feel bad. If a goal feels bad or makes us anxious, it's because we have decided to try to achieve it as the result of someone else's (for instance our parents', teachers', friends', or bosses') expectations of us. When we let go of what other people think and are being true to ourselves, our dreams and desires will always feel great!

Allowing ourselves to dream big keeps our life moving forward. As we think positively about all that we want, we emit high-frequency vibrations into the Universe that are specifically and exclusively ours. It is our choice to keep ourselves thinking thoughts that feel good so that we will rendezvous with the cooperative components that the Law of Attraction is lining up for us that will ultimately lead us to our desires.

Source

To me, Source is the creative energy of the universe. Source created the entire universe as well as our planet earth and everything on it.

We are extensions of Source in the physical body and, just like Source, we are powerful spiritual beings of loving, high-frequency, pure positive energy.

This is the essence of who we really are. I call this essence our inner being. Our inner being (or Source) is not only within us but also everywhere at once in the universe. It sees everything and since it is everywhere at once, it always has the broader perspective on our journey through life.

For instance, let's say we are standing on the top of a mountain and there are many paths we can take to get down the mountain. At the end of one of these paths is something we have wanted for a long time (e.g. a beautiful home, an ideal partner). The Source aspect of ourselves is everywhere at once so with its higher broader perspective of all the paths to choose from, it clearly knows the best path for us to take to reach our desired dream. However, in our physical bodies, on the ground, we can only see a few hundred feet ahead of us on each path winding down the mountain. We can't see the big picture like Source sees so we don't know which path to take. This is when listening to our inner being / gut instinct / intuition can really pay off.

Source communicates to us through our emotions and we can feel this communication in the area of our gut. This form of communication can also be called gut instinct, intuition, or inner guidance. I think it's one of the greatest gifts Source has given us. Whenever it's time to make a choice or a decision in which we are not sure what to do (like which path to take down the mountain that will support our desires), Source is there to guide us through our emotions. When our decisions feel good, Source is indicating to us that our decision is in alignment with what it knows will serve us. On the other hand, when our decisions feel bad or causes a knot in our stomach then that decision is out of alignment with what Source knows will provide the solution we want. Listening and understanding what our emotions are telling us takes practice, but the payoff is well worth it. Will we make choices that don't bring us what we want? Yes, but with practice we will learn to discern the difference between hearing our own inner voice and hearing the voice that pops into in our logical minds, that are formed from other peoples' opinions. Keep in mind that any choice that doesn't give us what we want is actually providing us a clarifying moment, so we can know more clearly what we do want. This is how we learn to have faith that Source is always here to support us and guide us towards our dreams, desires and highest joys.

Law of Attraction Principles Index

Principle	**Page**
Distraction Distraction temporarily will help you shift your vibration but to avoid repeating painful experiences we need to address buried emotional wounds and build new empowering habits of thought.	**9, 72**
Emotional Scale Recognize the pattern of thought that produces the emotion which keeps attracting what you don't want and purposefully choose thoughts that bring relief, small increments at a time to raise your vibration.	**XVI, 72**
Emotions guide us Our emotions are always guiding us. What we feel tells us what we are attracting, or more accurately, how the things we are attracting will feel when they arrive.	**XVI, 8, 35, 40, 41**
Everything is energy The Law of Attraction states simply that energy attracts like energy and according to physics, everything is energy. Our thoughts are energy (frequency) and thus are attractive in nature.	**XVI**
Faith When we release any and all doubt around the outcome of a choice we've made, we allow the Universe to bring us what we want in any number of delightful ways.	**36, 54**
Focus When we feel stuck in a rut, it's due to the powerful momentum of habitual thinking.	**35, 47, 59**
Habits The Law of Attraction supports any habit we choose whether it's empowering or not.	**6, 33, 73**

Principle	**Page**
Happiness You cannot attract a happy ending to an unhappy journey.	**45**
Influential Energy All forms of energy influence your vibrational atmosphere and resulting experiences. When you're not feeling good, relief can come by choosing to listen to others self-empowering or inspirational words.	**40, 55, 60**
Inspiration Inspired action steps come from your heart.	**62**
Instincts Gut instincts are part of the emotional guidance system we are born with. Paying attentions to our gut instincts can also be thought of as listening to our inner guidance or our inner being.	**8, 14, 35**
Intentions Pre-pave your experiences daily by setting your intentions about how you would like the results to feel before you embark on something.	**53**
Letting go Making peace with your current situation must be done before you can attract something better.	**36, 51**
Leverage Use the influential power of high frequency energy from other people to help you manifest your desires.	**40, 57, 72**
Mirroring The Law of Attractions works just like a mirror. The emotional essence of the energy we put out is always reflected back to us.	**26, 50, 76**

Principle	**Page**
Momentum Momentum influences the timing of manifestations. Every thought we think sends out a tiny burst of energy that also has a tiny amount of attractive power to it. Over time, the more we stay on a given idea, the more the momentum builds until we begin to attract physical things that reflect the essence of those thoughts.	**6, 24, 55, 59**
Passion The feeling of passion is the energy that creates our reality and when we're passionate about what we do, success and happiness follow.	**38**
Proof We create your own reality. New thoughts create a new life. Practicing this, over time, is the best way to prove to ourselves that the Law of Attraction exists.	**35, 36, 37, 54**
Reflection What goes around, comes around.	**50, 76**
Rendezvous We're continually being sent a stream of intuitive impulses that guide us and line us up with rendezvous equal to the emotions we are feeling. If we're feeling good, we'll rendezvous with good feeling persons, places, and events etc. When we're feeling bad, we rendezvous with things that don't feel good.	**XVII, 57**
Self-Acceptance Self-love and self-respect come before you can attract those that will love and respect you.	**76**
Solutions The key to attracting any solution is to stop looking at the problem.	**47, 57**

Resources and Suggested Reading Material

Business/Financial

Hill, Napoleon and Holden-Crowther, Ben, 2003. *Think and Grow Rich.* New York, NY: The Penguin Group.

Hicks, Esther and Jerry, 2008. *Money and the Law of Attraction: Learning to Attract Wealth, Health, and Happiness.* New York, NY: Hay House.

Family

Chapman, Gary, 2004. *The Five Love Languages: How to Express Heartfelt Commitment to Your Mate.* Chicago, IL: Northfield Publishing.

Mental Health

Shimoff, Marci, with Carol Kline, 2008. *Happy for No Reason.* New York, NY: Simon and Schuster.

Dyer, Dr. Wayne, 2004. *The Power of Intention.* New York, NY: Hay House.

Physical Health

Hay, Louise, 2004. *You Can Heal Your Life.* New York, NY: Hay House.

Northrup, Christiane, MD. 2006. *Women's Bodies, Women's Wisdom: Creating Physical and Emotional Health and Healing.* New York, NY: Bantam Dell.

Social Family

Carnegie, Dale, 1964. *How to Win Friends and Influence People.* New York, NY: Simon and Schuster.

Spiritual/Energy

Hicks, Esther and Jerry, 2004. *Ask and It Is Given: Learning to Manifest Your Desires.* New York, NY: Hay House.

Hicks, Esther and Jerry, 2010. *Getting into the Vortex: Guided Meditations.* New York, NY: Hay House.

Osteen, Joel, 2004. *Your Best Life Now: 7 Steps to Living at Your Full Potential.* New York, NY: Warner Faith.

Tolle, Eckhart, 2004. *The Power of Now: A Guide to Spiritual Enlightenment.* Novato, CA: New World Library.

Byrne, Rhonda, 2006. *The Secret.* New York, NY: Atria Books/Beyond Words Publishing.

Uplifting and empowering programs, such as TED Talks and Abraham-Hicks' teachings, can also be found on Hay House Radio and YouTube.

Acknowledgments

I want to extend my deep and sincere thanks to all the wonderful people in my life who have supported and encouraged me with writing this book.

Thank you to the love of my life, my husband Kevin. It was because of your encouragement that I stepped out of my comfort zone to explore becoming an author. Thank you for believing in me and supporting me from the minute I thought I might want to write a book. Your unwavering love and patience throughout the long three years of writing is truly appreciated.

I have so much love for my immediate family:

Thank you to my sisters, Kathy and Linda. I know you were both surprised to read about some of the things I'd experienced, which we'd never discussed as family members. You have both been there for me through all my painful life struggles, listening to me, encouraging me, and loving me unconditionally. Linda, I really appreciated watching you read the entire book on a warm summer day out on my patio, unable to put it down until you'd finished it!

Thank you to all my children, Kerri, Brian, Michael, and Jamie, for being the one constant joy in my life. Through it all you brought me consistent love and laughter!

A very big thank you goes to my daughter-in-law Marcie Carlson. You quickly read the entire book in just a few short days. Then you went over and beyond just reading it and took additional time to offer me helpful feedback and editing ideas.

I am blessed with many wonderful supportive friends:

Many thanks to my friend, Amelia Mimi Brown. Before it was even finished, you were the first person I asked to read my partial manuscript. Your enthusiasm and confidence that it would help many women inspired me to keep writing and get it done! Not only did you encourage me to become an author, but you also inspired me to become a professional speaker. You have shown us all that when we step into our fears, we allow ourselves to become all we're meant to be. Thank you!

Thank you to my longtime friend in UndercoverWear, Katie Nye. You were the role model and mentor I needed most when we first rendezvoused in the Wisconsin Dells. It changed my life! I value our deep friendship that grew from that point on. I truly appreciated all the hours you spent during your own personal vacation, to review my first draft! I will always remember our phone call where you reminded me that many women need to hear my story and will relate to, and benefit, from reading it. Your enthusiasm and support inspired me!

Many thanks to my good friend, Paul Flancbaum, for spending a full week out of your busy schedule reading and editing. I will always remember the day we sat down at your house and went through the entire manuscript together. You offered me a much-appreciated point of view from a male's perspective, and many great ideas on how to improve my writing style, punctuation and grammar.

Thank you to my longtime friend, Loree Sims, with whom I grew up. I'm grateful for our 50+ years of friendship and your eagerness to read my manuscript and share your valuable feedback. Thanks also to your wonderful husband, Presley, for asking you to read the entire book out loud as you drove across Florida on your long road trip. I appreciate that he enjoyed it so much that you didn't stop, even when your throat was exhausted from hours of reading out loud!

Thank you so much to my friend, Emily Gardner, whom I've known since 1976. You spent more hours than I can count, diligently reviewing my manuscript. Your expertise in the English language and your love of reading self-help and personal growth books was extremely useful. Your ongoing enjoyment of my message, even after reading the manuscript several times, really inspired me!

Thank you, Jodi Caltrider, whom I've known since 1981 when you joined my UndercoverWear team. From the time I met you, you always made it clear you didn't like reading books. So, twenty-five years later, your eagerness to read my book really surprised me, especially when you shared with me that you couldn't put it down. I appreciated your enthusiasm after reading it and that you even wanted me to write a few more chapters that would include our ongoing love story after our marriage. Your support inspired me to continue moving forward with sharing my story with the world.

Thank you, Tiffany James, CEO of UndercoverWear, for being a terrific role model as a businesswoman and a friend since 1981 and for your wise guidance and support for my personal growth throughout our many years together in UndercoverWear. As a result of your love and assistance at the end of my second marriage, I was able to begin to learn how to *step into a life of joy*, and now you have given me another memorable gift by writing the foreword to this, my first book. Thank you for always believing in me!

I also want to express my true appreciation and gratitude to my amazing editor, Sally Sutton, who's not only superbly talented at what she does but is funny, kind, and so wise. Because you are so familiar with the Law of Attraction and the Abraham-Hicks material, you have been a joy to work with. Your enthusiasm, positivity, supportive feedback, and suggestions as you went through the editing process continually confirmed that the Law of Attraction brought us together for a very good reason: co-creating at its best! Thank you for your continual support to help me launch my book's first edition in Kindle format.

Finally, I have a tremendous amount of gratitude for my wonderful friend, Susan Green. While reading my book, your hidden passion for proofreading emerged. Together we shared enjoyable deep discussions on how to make the revised second edition of *Stepping into a Life of Joy* more impactful and helpful for the readers. Thank you for the many months of time and effort that you gave from your heart!

To all the other wonderful souls that I haven't mentioned here who encouraged me and inspired me to finish my book – I truly love and appreciate you all!

Suzanne

About the Author

Suzanne C. Young is an intuitive life coach, mentor, author and inspirational speaker. Suzanne has worked with women for more than 30 years, helping them regain their sense of empowerment, confidence, and direction in life. She coaches individuals and groups, teaching concepts such as the Law of Attraction, spirituality, intuition, and being true to oneself.

As a professional speaker, Suzanne's programs include stress relief, mindfulness and meditation, Law of Attraction, improving relationships, and reconnecting with your Inner Guidance. The underlying message she conveys is always: when we change the quality of our thoughts, we change the quality of our lives.

She is also a contributing writer for Women2Women Michigan Magazine and featured as the cover story in their May 2017 issue. She is proud mother of four grown children and five grandchildren.

In her teaching autobiography, *Stepping Into a Life of Joy*, Suzanne shares how she developed her self-empowerment skills through a series of life-changing events as they related to the Law of Attraction. Her book is available in paperback and eBook at amazon.com.

Suzanne is also co-owner of Personal Success Programs with her husband Kevin. They offer intuitive life and business coaching, training programs, webinars, newsletters, workshops, and speaking engagements. For details on their work at Personal Success Programs, contact them at personalsuccessprograms.com.

35384386R00068

Made in the USA
Middletown, DE
10 February 2019